President Kennedy Fights the Cold War: The Bay of Pigs Invasion and the Cuban Missile Crisis

By Charles River Editors

Picture of the Bay of Pigs today

About Charles River Editors

Charles River Editors was founded by Harvard and MIT alumni to provide superior editing and original writing services, with the expertise to create digital content for publishers across a vast range of subject matter. In addition to providing original digital content for third party publishers, Charles River Editors republishes civilization's greatest literary works, bringing them to a new generation via ebooks.

Sign up here to receive updates about free books as we publish them, and visit Our Kindle Author Page to browse today's free promotions and our most recently published Kindle titles.

Introduction

Cuban leaders Fidel Castro and Che Guevara

The Bay of Pigs Invasion (April 17-19, 1961)

"Openly and unabashedly they are organizing training camps; openly and unabashedly they are building air bases and air strips. Everyone knows who is building the strips and buying planes, that mercenaries are recruiting troops. They even have the cynicism to publish photographs." – Fidel Castro, March 1961

Within just a month of becoming President, the issue of communist Cuba became central to John F. Kennedy and his administration. On February 3rd, 1961, President Kennedy called for a plan to support Cuban refugees in the U.S., and a month later, he created the Peace Corps, a program that trained young American volunteers to help with economic and community development in poor countries. Both programs were integral pieces of the Cold War and were attempts to align disadvantaged groups abroad with the United State and the West against the Soviet Union and its Communist satellites. Meanwhile, covert operations were laying the groundwork for overthrowing Cuban leader Fidel Castro, and he knew it. Castro railed against CIA involvement among Cubans trying to overthrow him and his still young revolution.

Matters came to a head that April, when the Kennedy Administration moved beyond soft measures to direct action. From April 17-20, 1,400 CIA-trained Cuban exiles landed on the beaches of Western Cuba in an attempt to overthrow Castro. This plan, known as the "Bay of Pigs," had been originally drafted by the Eisenhower Administration. The exiles landed in Cuba and were expected to be greeted by anti-Castro forces within the country, after which the U.S. would provide air reinforcement to the rebels and the Castro regime would slowly be overthrown.

From the onset, almost every phase of the operation went wrong. Ships were prevented from reaching shore by reefs previously thought to be seaweed beds on the basis of U-2 photographs. Antiquated American bombers missed a high percentage of their targets, and with American involvement already apparent to the world, the second round of air attacks was cancelled. Most of those who reached the beach in the land invasion were killed or captured, and the United States suffered immeasurable embarrassment on the international stage. On April 21st, in a White House press conference, President Kennedy accepted full responsibility for the failure, and over the following year, the U.S. and Cuba negotiated the release of the imprisoned exiles, who were finally released in December of 1962 in exchange for $55.5 million worth of food and medicine. The aborted invasion also became a nationalistic rallying cry for Castro, helping to consolidate public support in favor of his revolutionary government.

According to some, the invasion's famous name comes from a mistranslation for a type of fish found in the bay where the landing eventually occurred: the "Cochinos."[1] Regardless, the Bay of Pigs is viewed historically as one of the most ill-conceived and poorly executed covert paramilitary actions in the history of the United States, or as one historian put it, "the ultimate symbol of boneheaded interventionism."[2] More importantly, the failed invasion motivated Soviet leader Nikita Khrushchev to attempt to place medium range nuclear missiles in Cuba, due not only to his questioning of Kennedy's resolve but also to placate the concerns of Castro following the failed Bay of Pigs invasion. That would ultimately lead to the Cuban Missile Crisis in October 1962, arguably the closest the Cold War came to becoming a nuclear Armageddon.

President Kennedy Fights the Cold War comprehensively covers the planning that led to the fateful invasion. The origins of the campaign and the results and aftermath are also discussed. Along with pictures of important people, places, and events, you will learn about the Bay of Pigs like never before.

---

[1] J.A. Sierra, "Cuba in the 1960s: An Introduction" - www.history of cuba.com/history/havana/sixties.htm
[2] William Bradley, "Why We Should Miss John F. Kennedy 50 Years On" - www.huffingtonpost.com/william-bradley

A U.S. Navy patrol plane flying over a Soviet cargo ship during the crisis.

The Cuban Missile Crisis (October 1962)

"For, in the final analysis, our most basic common link is that we all inhabit this small planet. We all breathe the same air. We all cherish our children's future. And we are all mortal." – President John F. Kennedy, June 1963

When Kennedy came to power in 1961, Soviet leader Nikita Khrushchev was eager to test his mettle from the start, and Khrushchev's belief that he could push the inexperienced American leader around grew in the wake of the Bay of Pigs fiasco and the inconclusive Vienna summit in June 1961 that left Kennedy complaining to his brother Bobby that Khrushchev was "like dealing with Dad. All give and no take."

Motivated by the events of the previous year, 1962 saw Khrushchev made his most decisive decision. Still questioning Kennedy's resolve, and attempting to placate the concerns of Cuban leader Fidel Castro following the failed Bay of Pigs invasion, Khrushchev attempted to place medium range nuclear missiles in Cuba, just 90 miles off the coast of the United States. Though Castro warned him that the act would seem like an act of aggression to the Americans, Khrushchev insisted on moving the missiles in quietly, under the cover of darkness. These missiles could serve not only as a deterrent against any invasion of Cuba but also as the ultimate first-strike capability in the event of a nuclear war.

However, in October 1962, American spy planes discovered the Soviets were building nuclear missile sites in Cuba, and intelligence officials informed Kennedy of this on October 16th. It went without saying that nuclear missile sites located just miles off the coast of the American mainland posed a grave threat to the country, especially because missiles launched from Cuba would reach their targets in mere minutes. That would throw off important military balances in nuclear arms and locations that had previously ensured the Cold War stayed cold. Almost all senior American political figures agreed that the sites were offensive and needed to be removed, but how?

Ultimately, some of the biggest arguments during the crisis took place among members of the Kennedy administration and the military. Members of the U.S. Air Force wanted to take out the sites with bombing missions and launch a full-scale invasion of Cuba, but Kennedy and his brother feared that military action could ignite a full-scale escalation leading to nuclear war. Though he had previously taken aggressive stances on Cuba, Bobby was one of the voices who opposed outright war and helped craft the eventual plan: a blockade of Cuba. That was the decision President Kennedy ultimately reached as well, but it remained to be seen whether Khrushchev would test Kennedy's resolve yet again.

President Kennedy Fights the Cold War comprehensively covers the fateful days that brought the two superpowers closer to nuclear war than they had ever been before or would ever get again. The origins of the conflict and the confidential manner in which the crisis was defused are also discussed. Along with pictures of important people, places, and events, you will learn about the Cuban Missile Crisis like never before, in no time at all.

President Kennedy Fights the Cold War: The Bay of Pigs Invasion and the Cuban Missile Crisis

About Charles River Editors

Introduction

    Chapter 1: Khrushchev and Castro Come to Power

    Chapter 2: Plotting Against Castro

    Chapter 3: A New President

    Chapter 4: Action Before the Invasion

    Chapter 5: April 16-19

    Chapter 6: The Aftermath of the Failed Invasion

    Chapter 7: Kennedy and Khrushchev Meet at Vienna

    Chapter 8: Khrushchev Makes a Decision

    Chapter 9: U-2s Over Cuba

    Chapter 10: Kennedy Makes a Decision and a Speech

    Chapter 11: Implementing the Blockade and Reacting to It

    Chapter 12: An International Response

    Chapter 13: Finding a Way Out of the Crisis

    Chapter 14: The Aftermath of the Crisis

    Chapter 15: The Cuban Missile Crisis in Hindsight

Bibliography

Chapter 1: Khrushchev and Castro Come to Power

"Until Castro, the U.S. was so overwhelmingly influential in Cuba that the American ambassador was the second most important man, sometimes even more important than the Cuban president." - Earl T. Smith, former American Ambassador to Cuba, 1960

When Josef Stalin died in March 1953, the Soviet Union found itself leaderless for the first time in decades, and after 30 years under the absolute control of one fearsome figure, a power struggle was inevitable. The men who headed the Soviet Union were all intensely ambitious and, having survived Stalin, crafty, ruthless survivors. Ultimately, it was a career Communist official, Nikita Khrushchev, who reached the top and filled the vacuum of power in January 1955 after several top officials were purged.

Khrushchev

For all of his prominence and power within the Soviet Union, Khrushchev was a virtual unknown in the outside world, and the West was less than impressed to say the least. Looking at the short, heavyset Russian who wore ill-fitting suits, Khrushchev was dismissed as a buffoon. British Foreign Secretary Harold Macmillan labeled him a "fat, vulgar man" and predicted he would not last long.

However, the "buffoon" soon showed the West he was not to be trifled with. At every turn, Khrushchev took the tactic of confrontation over conciliation. A believer in the ultimate superiority of the Soviet System, Khrushchev wanted to position the Soviet Union as a player on the world stage, an equal to the Western Allies—particularly the United States. His view was summarized in a statement made to Western diplomats at the Polish Embassy in Moscow: "We will bury you." Khrushchev didn't appear to be engaging in hyperbole either; the statement came as Soviet forces were crushing an uprising in Hungary that led to the deaths of nearly 4,000 Hungarians.

This confrontational persona was quite at odds with how Khrushchev would later be described by a biographer ("He could be charming or vulgar, ebullient or sullen, he was given to public displays of rage (often contrived) and to soaring hyperbole in his rhetoric. But whatever he was, however he came across, he was more human than his predecessor or even than most of his foreign counterparts, and for much of the world that was enough to make the USSR seem less mysterious or menacing.").

One of the first fights Khrushchev chose to pick was over West Berlin and a divided Germany. He demanded in November 1958 that the Western Allies complete a peace treaty with both Germanys and the Soviet Union, or he would conclude a separate treaty with East Germany giving the Soviet satellite control over the routes to the city. While the Western Allies were divided over the issue, Khrushchev repeatedly extended the deadline, indicating he had no real stomach for conflict himself. Eventually, this would lead to a summit on the issue of Berlin that would be both a disaster and one that would affect a future summit between Khrushchev and Kennedy in 1961.

Khrushchev also aimed to directly challenge the United States militarily, ardent in the belief that more nuclear missiles would help defend the Soviet Union. He turned away from conventional ground forces and a large ocean-going navy by increasing production of missiles. Soviet eagerness to develop an intercontinental ballistic missile (ICBM) was fueled in part by the superiority of the U.S. Air Force, which was larger and more advanced than the Soviet arsenal. Thus, the Soviet Union felt it needed alternative ways to deliver nuclear warheads into American territory if its nuclear arsenal were to remain strategically relevant and military equity or superiority was to be achieved. The creation of the ICBM essentially negated the superiority of the U.S. Air Force, erasing all strategic edges the U.S. held over the USSR. At the same time, with this success, the Soviets opened nearly a decade of dominance of space exploration, which culminated in the launching of the world's first human being into outer space.

Khrushchev also spurred on the Soviet space program, which, unknown to the rest of the world, was actually making great strides. The Soviets had few missiles in spite of Khrushchev's public boasting of a large and varied ballistic missile program. While the world was skeptical, one event changed that into real fear and concern: the launch of Sputnik. Thanks to its transmission, and the bright mark it created in nighttime skies across the world, the world was already aware of the launch and orbit of Sputnik-1 before the Soviets formally announced the successful launch and orbit of their satellite. Naturally, the West wasn't thrilled to learn about the Soviets' launch of the first artificial object into Earth's orbit. Sputnik-1 could be measured in inches, but that large rocket it was attached to could wreak havoc if equipped with a nuclear warhead. Moreover, if Americans could see Sputnik-1, they were justifiably worried Sputnik-1 could see them.

From a political standpoint, the success of Sputnik helped convince the world that Khrushchev was willing to walk the walk, not just talk the talk. This led to political and policy ramifications in the United States; a major theme in the late 1950s, and particularly in the 1960 election, was the "missile gap", a gap which, when combined with the Space Race, provided politicians on both sides of the political spectrum in the United States with an argument to increase federal spending in research and development, science and technology education, and the creation of a space program. All this occurred as a public response to the new Soviet threat, but privately, American leaders knew (thanks to U-2 spy planes) that the Soviet missile and space programs were less advanced than the bellicose Khrushchev indicated in speech after speech.

After Vice President Richard Nixon visited Russia and Khrushchev visited America, President Dwight D. Eisenhower planned to visit Moscow in 1960, but that visit would never take place, because on May 1, 1960 Soviet surface-to-air missiles shot down a U-2 spy plane piloted by Francis Gary Powers. Khrushchev held off announcing the shoot down until May 5, worried that the incident would jeopardize a summit about Berlin scheduled for May 15, and when the announcement was made, Khrushchev tried to blame the flights on rogue elements in the U.S. military, attempting to deflect possible blame from Eisenhower. The President, however, admitted that the flights had occurred and that he had ordered them, which put Khrushchev in a very difficult position with the summit approaching.

Gary Powers (right) in front of a U-2

The Paris Summit that month ended up being a disaster. When he arrived, Khrushchev demanded an apology from Eisenhower and a promise of no more U-2 flights. He got no apology, but Eisenhower had already suspended the flights and offered his Open Skies proposal for mutual overflight rights. Khrushchev refused and left the summit, and Eisenhower's visit to the Soviet Union was cancelled.

The collapse of the Paris Summit brought out an even more bellicose side of the Soviet premier. In his September 1960 visit to the U.N. General Assembly, which took place just two months before Kennedy won a close presidential election against Nixon, Khrushchev showed his "hard approach". Rather than trying to charm the West, he began the Soviet Union's wooing of the new Third-World countries in an effort to bring them into the Soviet orbit. Of course, that effort was largely forgotten thanks to Khrushchev's personal histrionics. During a speech by a Filipino delegate criticizing the Soviet Union for decrying colonialism while engaging in it, he took off his shoe and began banging it repeatedly on his table while calling the speaker a "jerk, stooge, and lackey", as well as "a toady of American imperialism". When the Romanian Foreign Vice-Minister began vocally attacking the Filipino delegate, his microphone was cut off, leading to jeers among Eastern bloc members. The meeting was immediately adjourned, with Assembly President Frederick Boland slamming his gavel down so hard that the head broke off and went flying.

Khrushchev at the U.N. in September 1960

Around the same time that Khrushchev came to power in the Soviet Union, the balance of power changed in Cuba. Today, most Americans are well aware of the country's ongoing issues with Cuba, and the critical role played by Cuban leader Fidel Castro, but naturally, the complicated nature of Cuba's history is far less known. Before Castro's successful revolution, Fulgencio Batista emerged from the military to take power in Cuba in 1934, and in 1940 he was elected President after earning a popular vote of 60%. However, in later years, when his hand-picked successor was defeated in a national election, he dispensed with the idea of a democratic process altogether, overthrew the constitution and the government of President Carlos Prio, and set himself up as dictator of Cuba.

Batista

Fidel Castro was not the first or only revolutionary who sought to overthrow the Batista government. Born in 1926, he came out of the Catholic school system in Havana, where he earned a degree in law from the University of Havana. His alignment with the Ortodoxo party (a social-democratic party) did not set him so much between the concepts of communism and democracy, at least not to the outside world, but with a directed intent against what he perceived as a Batista dictatorship that had produced widespread poverty and an enormous gap between the wealthy and the poverty-stricken.

Despite his strong opposition, few could have predicted that 26 year old Fidel Castro would pose the first serious and violent challenge to the legitimacy of strongman Fulgencio Batista's rule. Along with his brother Raúl and other allies, Fidel began to stockpile weapons and organize a secret opposition movement known as "The Movement", which had both civil and military committees. The conspirators chose the Moncada barracks of Santiago, one of the country's largest military garrisons, as the target of their audacious assault on the ruling regime. The plan was to catch the garrison during a holiday, when much of its active force would be away, seizing allowing them to seize control of it and weaken the army's strategic hold on the province. In the meantime, they hoped, a popular revolt would emerge in support of their efforts.

In military terms, the attack on the Moncada Barracks on July 26, 1953 was a catastrophic failure, perhaps unsurprisingly for a leader with no military experience. Poorly armed and badly outnumbered, the rebels were routed, and some of them never even reached the barracks. Of Castro's approximately 160 companions, 60 were killed in the assault and dozens more were captured and tortured to death by Batista's police. Castro himself, along with his brother Raúl and a number of his closest associates, was captured, tried, and imprisoned. Naturally, Batista used the events to crack down further on his political opponents, including members of the Ortodoxo.

Nevertheless, the attack proved to be a political watershed and the true origin of Fidel Castro's successful revolutionary career, even if not in the way he initially intended. His trial in particular would provide Castro with a highly public platform from which to galvanize popular sentiment against Batista. The speech he delivered at his trial was subsequently published in a series of sold-out editions and became the manifesto for what became known as the July 26 Movement. In the speech, he declared, "I know that jail will be as hard as it has ever been for anyone, filled with threats, with vileness, and cowardly brutality; but I do not fear this, as I do not fear the fury of the miserable tyrant who snuffed out the life of seventy brothers of mine. Condemn me, it does not matter. History will absolve me!" The defiant final line of the speech echoed across the Cuban political landscape for decades.

Fidel Castro under arrest after the Moncada attack.

In the summer of 1955, after a resounding victory in an election widely regarded as fraudulent, Batista chose to pardon and release the 26 of July Movement leaders. The choice may seem surprising, but Batista was under pressure to avoid the appearance of dictatorship and illegitimacy. Furthermore, he was evidently quite confident after the election in the solidity of his status and regarded Castro and his allies as little more than a distraction, not a major threat.

Fidel did not stay long in Cuba after his release. His vocal activism was enough to give Batista second thoughts a mere month after the amnesty was signed. Anti-government violence had broken out across Havana, and although it was not clear Castro had much of a leadership role in any of it, he wrote articles and gave radio-broadcasted speeches supporting and encouraging it. Batista had resorted to extrajudicial assassinations previously, and Castro and his supporters began to fear for their lives in the climate of violence that took hold over the summer. On June 24, 1955, Raúl Castro fled Cuba for Mexico, and his older brother followed on July 7.

In the early months of 1956, supporters of Castro's Movimiento 26 de Julio began to converge in Mexico City from Cuba and various places of exile. Castro, based in Mexico since his exile began, had begun secretly planning a rebel military invasion of the island, which was to occur later that same year. Now was the time to gather his men and start preparing them to take on Batista's much larger and better-equipped army. It would have been an insane proposition had Castro and his inner circle still not been firmly convinced despite their previous failures that the Cuban populace would ultimately rally to their side against the government.

Shortly after arriving in Cuba on December 2, 1956, Castro and his 82 companions were caught in an ambush, and most were killed or captured. Remarkably, though, the leaders of the group survived and reunited once the chaos had subsided, including the Castro brothers, Che Guevara, and a few others. They fled into the high, treacherous, and thickly forested Sierra Maestra mountain range that runs alongside Cuba's southern coast. Che would write that these days were "the most painful days of the war".

Che in Las Villas province, Cuba, November 1958.

The first stage of operations having failed miserably, the rebels moved on to the second set of tasks of the insurgency: building a network of support among the local peasantry, recruiting new fighters, and establishing connections with sympathetic groups in other parts of the country. In all of these areas they proved more successful. Already by the end of December, they had begun to train locals who wanted to join the revolutionary force. The impoverished and marginal peasantry of the Sierra Maestra had little access to education, electricity, or medical care, and the promises of equality and redistribution put forth by the rebels had an obvious resonance with many of them. Their knowledge of the countryside was an invaluable resource, as none of the invaders had much familiarity with the territory.

From their inauspicious beginnings, the rebels did gradually expand their operations through recruitment, alliance, and growing support from the populace. A pivotal moment came in March 1957, when an affiliated group of urban guerrillas attempted to storm the Presidential Palace and assassinate Batista. The effort ended in failure, but it also seemed to signal the weakness and vulnerability of the regime, and it galvanized opposition among the public, which largely sympathized with the would-be assassins. The situation was exacerbated by the increasing brutality Batista unleashed against anyone suspected of involvement in subversive activity.

Batista's illegitimacy and weakness was confirmed when the United States withdrew support from his government and imposed sanctions to express disapproval of the chaos and violence that now consumed Cuba. Through the same period, the guerrillas took all measures they could to consolidate their legitimacy in the eyes of Cubans and the international community. On the latter front, they were helped when *New York Times* journalist Herbert Matthews sought them out in February 1957. Matthews published an extensive and sympathetic interview with Castro, which placed him in the eyes of the world as an idealistic, authoritative, and morally serious freedom fighter who, Matthews assured his readers, had no affiliation with communism.

By early 1958, the rebels had successfully beaten back a number of relatively small incursions by Batista's forces, who were nevertheless always more numerous than their opponents. As it turned out, Batista was not one to hold on doggedly to power. On the night of December 31, 1958, he fled the country with his closest allies and a large sum of cash and headed to the Dominican Republic. Upon leaving, he named Judge Carlos Manuel Piedra as president and Cantillo as head of the armed forces, but few in Cuba were paying attention to these developments: all were awaiting the next move of the *barbudos*, the bearded rebels whose exploits had now captured the imagination of the country. Upon hearing the news of the dictator's departure, Che Guevara and Camilo Cienfuegos set out for Havana, where they arrived on January 2. Fidel Castro had orders for them: each was to take over one of the major military garrisons of the city. Fidel had already made a series of decisions about the initial transition of power, all of which suggested a cautious desire to establish a distance from the more radical politics espoused by Che and Raúl, among others. Discarding Batista's last-ditch appointments, he selected his own transitional president and prime minister: the moderate Manuel Urrutia, a liberal lawyer with international connections, and José Miró. Fidel reserved the position of commander in chief of the armed forces for himself.

Fidel received a public hero's welcome when he arrived in the capital on January 8, 1959, and he initially tried to use his folk hero status to work as a unifying force, staying aloof from the initial wranglings of the provisional government. At the same time, immediately following the takeover of Havana, Castro executed over 700 Batista supporters by firing squad. This further unsettled the American government, but Castro compared his actions to the dropping of atomic bombs on Hiroshima and Nagasaki, citing that those civilians, unlike Batista followers, were innocent.

By February, Castro was mired in implacable conflict with the transitional leadership he had helped appoint, and he now essentially insisted that they defer to his authority on controversial matters. Now in a more central and visible role, Castro began to steer things more clearly in a radical, communist direction, but he was still concerned about America to the north and hoped to avoid an enmity that already seemed inevitable once Castro systematically alienated the moderates and liberals who had not long before been his allies.

Indeed, American relations with the new regime, which it reluctantly recognized in the beginning, was troubled from the start. Part of the American problem with Castro replacing Batista was the former dictator's status as an excellent facilitator for U.S. corporations in Cuba, as sugar companies and other enterprises grew rich from the island's resources despite the disadvantages experienced by the general populace. Then, in March 1960, *Le Coubre*, a French ship carrying Belgian arms, exploded in the harbor at Havana, killing about 100 and wounding about 300. At funeral services on the following day, Castro immediately accused the CIA of sabotaging the ship with the aim of blaming the Cuban regime.

President Dwight D. Eisenhower personally had no use for the new head of Cuban government, and he went to great lengths to minimize his importance. For example, Eisenhower went out to play golf during Castro's April visit to Washington, directing him instead to meet with Vice President Richard Nixon. When Nixon asked Castro about the probability of elections in Cuba, Castro replied frankly that the people didn't want elections. When asked about the executions, he answered that they were the result of the people's will. Nixon took such answers to mean that Castro would too easily follow mob sentiment. According to Volume 3 of the CIA's declassified archives, Nixon took a heightened personal interest in the Castro issue, "intervening in the planning of the invasion on behalf of William Pawley (top Republican and Nixon campaign contributor), a wealthy businessman with 'enterprises' in Cuba."[3]

---

[3] CIA Official History of the Bay of Pigs Operation - www.paperlessarchives.com/bay_of_pigs_cia_history.html

Eisenhower

Nixon

    Many in the American government, Nixon chief among them, were even more uncomfortable with Castro's declaration of "neutrality" in the Cold War. The Eisenhower administration had already experienced similar statements from leaders around the world like Egypt's Gamal Abdel Nasser, and the administration was put off by Castro's association with Che. With Che now de facto head of the Cuban economy, he and Castro began to propose its reorganization along lines even more radical than the communist economies of the Eastern Bloc had attempted: they wished to replace wage labor altogether with an ethic of work driven entirely by "moral incentives," in which all commitment to individual advancement and personal wealth would disappear in favor of a devotion to collective social well-being. Cuba's wealth began to flow out of the country along with a large part of the upper and middle class.

Fidel and Che marching in Havana, 1960

In retaliation for the perceived slights, Castro nationalized all American property, most importantly the sugar corporations. He further nationalized the telephone exchange and banks, limiting communication with the mainland. By the time Eisenhower reduced the economic exchange with Cuba by 85% (the cigar industry by 95%), Castro had already turned to the Soviet Union, which agreed to buy the sugar rejected by the U.S. and fund many of his central programs, including the "war on illiteracy" and free universal health care. When Soviet tankers brought their crude oil for refining in Cuba during the same months, Texaco, Esso and Shell all refused to accept the cargo. These events rankled the Eisenhower administration and inspired the U.S. to begin the training of anti-Castro exiles to retake the island. Castro took Eisenhower's mounting economic pressure against central Cuban businesses, such as the sugar and cigar industries, to mean that the U.S. had "declared economic war on Cuba."[4] With the United States and its European allies now hardened in their hostility to the new government, Cuba signed a comprehensive trade pact with the Soviet Union in February 1960.

Chapter 2: Plotting Against Castro

Eisenhower had discussed anti-Castro programs since the fall of 1959, hoping to assemble a secretive regimen of harassment that would make Castro's downfall appear to be a result of his own mistakes. Furthermore, long before the Bay of Pigs invasion, Cuban groups were already

---
[4] National Security Archives

conducting sea raids out of Florida, and anti-Castro elements in Cuba were conducting acts of sabotage against public gatherings and targets of infrastructure. Private bombing raids from the mainland were destroying massive numbers of *arrobas* (a weight equivalent to 25 pounds) of sugar cane on a regular basis, and by March 1960, plantations were set afire around Havana and in other provinces by internal resistance groups.

Despite international knowledge of past American activities, such as the successful Guatemalan overthrow and the ousting of Iranian prime minister Mohammed Massadegh in 1953, coupled with a certainty that Castro understood the U.S. pattern of regime change, the Eisenhower Administration's attempts to conduct subterfuge of this sort continued. Castro hoped to diffuse the attempts through public statements that clearly indicated his degree of knowledge. In a speech presented later in March 1960, he declared that "if there is an invasion, the war, they can be sure, will be to the death."[5] Ambassador Pedro Martinez Fraga echoed Castro's certainty two months later in a public declaration, also made in the United Nations, indicating that he could "guarantee categorically that Guatemalan territory is being used at this very time with the complicity of President Ydigoras and the assistance of United Fruit, as a bridgehead for an invasion of our country."[6]

Support within the CIA for conducting concrete anti-Castro actions was greatly aided by the presence of Manuel Francisco Artime Buesa, a former member of Castro's revolutionary army who had become an exile in the U.S. As an expatriate leader, he fit the CIA's bill perfectly by being of anti-nationalization conviction, insisting that all American property should be returned to its rightful owners, and supporting virtually all of the assassination plans discussed within the agency during the early 1960s. Artime served in the Cuban exile force, Brigade 2506, and after relocating to the U.S. after his release, became responsible for setting up four anti-Castro bases in Costa Rica and Nicaragua. Before long, hundreds of paramilitary recruits were directed through him, a small navy was established, planes were procured, and a significant amount of American weaponry was stockpiled. After Castro nationalized the banks, businesses and public services in December of 1959, Artime referred to the growing regime as a "criollo Kremlin"[7] that was intent on deceiving its populace as to the elimination of private property and personal choice.

---

[5] National Security Archives
[66] National Security Archives
[7] National Security Archives

Artime saluting as he stands near President Kennedy and the First Lady in December 1962

In February of 1960, Artime, leader of the Movimento de Recuperacion Revolucinario, had released the basic points of his anti-Castro intentions, entitled "Idearo Puntos Basicos." In the preamble, he wrote that the intention was not only to overthrow Castro, "but to permanently fight for an ideology of Christ...to liberate the nation so treacherously sold to the Communist International."[8] In this same month, Soviet official Anastas Mikoyan visited Cuba, publicly stating in his report that "the USSR has shifted from cautious attitude to one of active support."[9]

It is not difficult to see why the United States reacted differently to Castro than it had to other dictatorships in the region. Certainly, such proximity to American shores was unsettling, but in addition, following the Cuban revolution, Castro never again spoke in public without an

---
[8] National Security Archives
[9] National Security Archives

emotion-laden tirade delivered against the United States. His behavior was, at least to Americans' ears, "arrogant, insolent and provocative."[10] Indeed, by the time America's relationship with Castro was more fully developed, many in the U.S. government came to believe that "Castro was insane...a complete hysteric with a messianic complex."[11] In a further shock, the island of Cuba, which had always seemed to Americans as little more "than a place of tropical promiscuity,"[12] had now become a haven for earnest American opposition, increasingly throwing itself into the arms of the United States' greatest foe. In this sense, Castro's revolution and the larger Soviet plan for communist revolutions across the globe came to be seen as one and the same.

A failed contract had already been put on Castro's life in 1959, and it was not the only such action to fail over the ensuing years, whether originating with corporations, governments or the world of organized crime. Of course, these were all done under the radar, and further impeding an official U.S. response was the popularity in which Castro was held by the American population. The majority of Americans were "still in love with the Cuban revolutionaries...both Castro and Guevara seen as romantic freedom fighters."[13] Such a glamorous view would persist among young Americans for awhile, in part because Castro had not completely revealed his communist leanings and seemingly spent much of his energies upgrading everyday life in Cuba. Thus, in order for American officials to proceed with public support, this heroic imagery had to first be shattered.

Based on Nixon's recommendations, Eisenhower formulated a plan which was initially entitled "A Program of Covert Action Against the Castro Regime." Such a program depended on (a) a collective opposition, unified among Cuban exiles, primarily those living in the United States; (b) a functional intelligence effort within Cuba; and (c) the development of a paramilitary force that would successfully disguise its American origins. The resulting mission would come to cost approximately $46 million after an initial estimate of about $13 million, but the larger figure was still considered an acceptable cost by the Eisenhower administration. A less far-reaching mission had been proposed by Allen Dulles, Director of the CIA, recommending various acts of sabotage against the sugar industry, but Eisenhower was already resolved on the total removal of Castro and requested that the agency come back with a more inclusive outline to that end. Present at the meeting were Vice-President Nixon, Acting Secretary of State Douglas Dillon, the Secretary of the Treasury, and Acting Chair of the Joint Chiefs of Staff, General Lyman Lemnitzer. The outgoing president was pleased with the resulting coordination between armed forces and government agencies, maintaining only an insistence that all possible traces of American involvement be eliminated from the public and world view.

---

[10] Louis A. Pérez, Jr., "Fear and Loathing of Fidel Castro: Sources of US Policy toward Cuba", in *Journal of Latin American Studies*, Vol. 34 No. 2, May 2002, p. 230
[11] Louis A. Pérez, Jr., p. 230
[12] Louis A. Pérez, Jr., p. 230
[13] www.marxists.org/history/cuba/subject/bay-of-pigs/index.htm

This plan was the first specifically outlined action to emerge, but several alternate plans involved the simultaneous overthrow of Castro and the Dominican Republic's General Rafael Trujillo. At one point, the CIA hoped to eliminate three major figures, and the agency inquired of an agent in Havana whether he was "sufficiently motivated to risk arranging an accident for Raul Castro, and offering ten thousand dollars for its successful completion."[14] However, the agent was not enthusiastic and disappeared from contact. More specifically, recent declassified documents from the National Security Archives outline Eisenhower's plan along with a chapter entitled "Propaganda Plan in Support of Military Forces."[15] The specific mission categories included the intention to "maintain morale of anti-Castro forces...instruct pro-patriot forces...intimidate Castro forces...present desired picture...to world opinion...counteract Sino-Soviet propaganda...appeal to other governments for support...instruct individuals on how and where they can join...instruct the populace how to fight in place...tactical instructions to patriot forces without communication channels...provoke fence-sitters into joining 'the winning side.'"[16]

Raul Castro and Che Guevara during the revolution

Diplomatic relations with Cuba were broken nine months after approval of the Nixon/Eisenhower plan, and Eisenhower waited for the proper moment in which to launch the invasion, hoping, according to some, that the right opportunity would avail itself to allow an administration with a greater military background to accomplish the task. Eisenhower was more

---
[14] The National Security Archive
[15] The National Security Archive
[16] The National Security Archive

than willing to move against Castro during his presidency, "before Kennedy's inauguration, if 'a really good excuse' was provided by Castro."[17] Eisenhower even seemed willing to instigate such an opportunity if Castro did not present a visible opening, and he was quoted as saying, "Failing that, perhaps we could think of manufacturing something that would be generally acceptable." Although this would suggest that administration actions had not yet been taken, covert arms shipments were already being air-dropped. An indication of failures to come, the first massive drop of weaponry missed its target by seven miles and landed on a dam, only to be picked up by Castro forces. The receiving Cuban agent was immediately apprehended and shot. On top of that, the plane got lost returning from the drop and was forced to land in Mexico instead of Guatemala. The aircraft and crew were released back to the CIA after a great degree of diplomatic difficulty.

Chapter 3: A New President

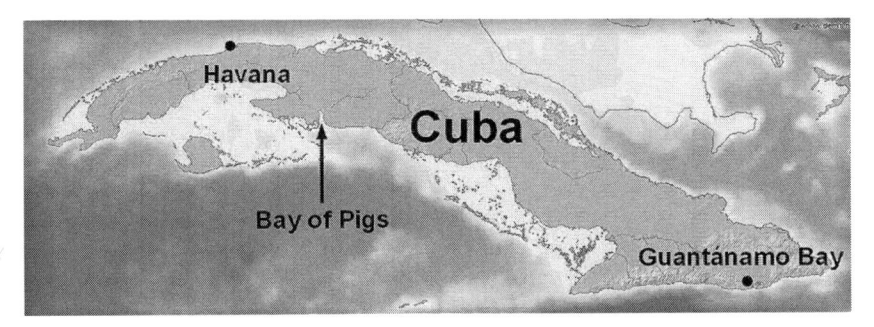

Map of Cuba and the location of the Bay of Pigs

Despite Nixon's eagerness to proceed, Eisenhower's "opportunity" never did come about, and when new President John F. Kennedy was briefed on the plan shortly after the inauguration, certain elements were omitted at Nixon's suggestion. The new president adopted the plan, at least in terms of outward rhetoric, having made "serious commitments" to Cuban exiles during the campaign. Kennedy was somewhat bound as well by his previous criticisms of Eisenhower's handling of the situation, often reciting the prophetically recurrent theme in speeches, "If you can't stand up to Castro, how can you be expected to stand up to Khrushchev?"[18]

---

[17] www.marxists.org
[18] The National Security Archive

Kennedy

Among the great fallacies shared by the two administrations was the fantasy that such an operation could remain covert with the absence of any clearly-marked U.S. military personnel. Another was the misguided belief that the specific U.S. plan could remain secret despite so many preparatory activities being shared between such a large number of people in various American and Latin American locations. On October 30, 1960, Cuban Prime Minister Raul Roa openly expressed knowledge of American "mercenaries and revolutionaries" being trained in Guatemalan camps, and his public expressions were accurate to a fault. The U.S. paid no heed to such revelations and continued its training of exiles. Of the force of 1,400, 200 were former soldiers for Batista, and 14 were wanted for murder in Cuba. The first 300, however, had already begun their training in the United States and the Canal Zone, shifting to Guatemala following an agreement with President Miguel Ydigoras. Eager to proceed, neither administration inwardly admitted that their hopes for secrecy were all but shot long before implementation of the plan. Putting the mission in further peril, crucial last minute logistical alterations continued to be made all the way up until the very last minute, most notably the decision to move the landing site to a swamp on the southern coast rather than at the nearby port of Trinidad. Kennedy feared that recognition of a high-profile American presence would cause problems with Soviet relations in Europe, and as a result, America's might would be stifled from fully assisting what was to appear as Cubans liberating Cubans. As late as April 12, five days before the invasion, the president was still trying to maintain secrecy by holding firm in a press conference that America had "no intention of intervening in Cuban affairs."[19]

Kennedy's preoccupation with American secrecy (shared by and inherited from Eisenhower) might have seemed possible in the moment, given the limited scope of the initial landing. After all, the landing location did not, in the President's mind, require a large town or complete harbor, only the ability to hold a beach. No matter the topography or boundaries of the captured area, a provisional government would be announced, with its "capital" to be immediately established on that spot. This new government, however fragile or bogus, would immediately request military assistance from the United States, and such a request would appear internationally legal (if not suspiciously unethical). American forces could then respond in full, sweeping the Castro regime away with support from the newly liberated Cuban population.

The landing would, as an integral part of the plan (at least in the CIA's vision), be covered by an "air umbrella" of jet fighters. However, a tragic misunderstanding persisted between the White House and the CIA, which believed that the bulk of the action was to be taken primarily from the air. In the end, a failure to mutually understand intentions between the President and the CIA may have been the plan's greatest problem - "The Bay of Pigs was approved because the CIA and White House assumed they were speaking the same language, when, in fact, they were speaking in utterly different tongues."[20] Richard Bissell, Deputy Director of Operations, expressed great astonishment that the whole affair was to be conducted by a central amphibious invasion in the dead of night, an action which he believed had only been attempted successfully once since World War I. Bissell believed that the entire administration was beset with an "infectious optimism,"[21] intoxicated with the hope that Castro's forced would become immediately deflated and that the modest Cuban air defenses would be destroyed at the onset. When orders descended from Bissell to subordinate Jack Esterline, one of the underlings in charge of operations close to the actual fighting, he replied "...this is not my kind of capability."[22] For this reason, Colonel Jack Hawkins of the U.S. Marines was brought in.

---

[19] U.S. History.com/Bay of Pigs Invasion
[20] Piero Gleijeses, "Ships in the Night: The CIA, the White House and the Bay of Pigs", in *Journal of Latin American Studies*, Vol. 27, No. 1, February 1995: Cambridge, p. 2
[21] www.marxist.org
[22] Piero Gleijeses, p. 10

Bissell

Perhaps not surprisingly, Eisenhower, the architect of the amphibious landings on D-Day, was naturally enamored of the amphibious landing, but his attempts at secrecy meant very little of the plan or communications between participants were put to paper, which caused problems for the incoming Kennedy administration. As it turned out, the information gulf was extraordinary, even as the military and the Kennedy administration seemed to think everything was mutually understood. The military, according to later declassified CIA documents, "had one idea of this invasion...they [at the top] missed the point completely. All we were going to do was to go in there, take a beachhead big enough to protect an airfield, and let the planes do their work."[23] One of the biggest reasons for the miscommunication was that the transition from Eisenhower to Kennedy didn't fully spell out Eisenhower's plan. Furthermore, former members of the Eisenhower administration offered little or no assistance to the new White House once Kennedy decided to go ahead. Furthermore, additional problems had to be dealt with, including an uprising in Guatemala that threatened the existence and viability of American air bases in the country.

Kennedy's Cabinet did not unanimously support the plan, and Secretary of State Chester Bowles rejected it on moral and ethical grounds: "We would be deliberately violating the fundamental obligations we assumed in the Act of Bogota establishing the Organization of American States."[24] Senator William J. Fulbright was outspoken in his opposition to a potential invasion, believing that "the operation was wildly out of proportion to the threat."[25] However, Kennedy's optimism was understandable given his recent record. He seemed to have the Midas touch by being nominated and elected against the odds, and he was viewed by many as euphoric

---

[23] Grafton L. Lynch, Central Intelligence Agency - Bay of Pigs Release - Aug., 2, 2011 - www/foia.cia.gov/collection/bay-of-pigs-release, p. xi
[24] www.marxist.org
[25] www.marxist.org

in his intent to replace the Cuban regime. Since the CIA-aided revolution had been so successful in Guatemala, much of that action served as a model. Furthermore, the CIA had conducted the re-installation of a Caribbean-wide radio signal originating from Greater Swan Island, as well as a complete refurbishing of the airfield to make it accessible. From there, broadcasts could be heard throughout the larger region, especially by Cuban citizens the Kennedy administration believed could be persuaded to join in a reshaping of their government. In a sense, the radio transmissions "became the symbol of the anti-Castro front."[26]

Ahead of the invasion, the CIA joined with the Frente Revolucinario Democrático junta, and leadership positions were filled with CIA choices from the early '50s. Strangely, the Director of Intelligence was not fully included in the loop during any phases of preparation; instead, Director of Plans Richard Helms and Deputy Frank Wisner were far more well-informed. A trio of immediate subordinates were left directly in charge at the ground level: Jack Esterline, Colonel Hawkins and Colonel Stanley Beerli.

As a result, the combination of Kennedy's inexperience, the previous administration's unwillingness to offer enough detailed information on the plan, and sudden last minute alterations to the plan all contributed to a spotty effort that sabotaged coordination and mutual awareness. As later declassified CIA documents put it, the mission "might have succeeded only if air operations plans by the CIA had been retained intact,"[27] and that the "distortion of those plans...insured the establishment of the first communist government in the Western Hemisphere."[28]

Chapter 4: Action Before the Invasion

By December 12, 1960, the American propaganda campaign was in full bloom, with private planes from the United States dropping anti-Castro leaflets over numerous Cuban cities. By January 14, 1961, travel of American citizens to Cuba was prohibited, and a month later, the progression toward an invasion accelerated. The CIA, based on Eisenhower's preference for a large amphibious landing, brought the Trinidad Plan to Kennedy, calling for a mixed landing with heavy air assault in the harbor of Trinidad. The safety valve was a hope that if the invasion failed in any aspect, the troops could take refuge in the Escambray Mountains and act like a guerilla unit, in much the same way Castro's forces had during their overthrow of Batista. In a continuing desire to minimize the American profile, Kennedy rejected that plan as too "spectacular."[29]

In fact, Kennedy's hope for secrecy had already been reduced to shambles by the previous August, as the *Miami Herald* published stories of the CIA training Cuban exiles in Florida.

---
[26] Piero Gleijeses, p. 6
[27] Central Intelligence Agency, p. 1
[28] Central Intelligence Agency, p. 1
[29] National Security Archives

Those exiles spoke with considerable abandon considering they were members of a secret mission. *The New York Times* followed suit a few months later by publishing Paul Kennedy's report, "US helps Train Anti-Castro Force at Secret Guatemalan Base." Meanwhile, Castro railed against CIA involvement among Cubans trying to overthrow him and the still young revolution. In March 1961, he spoke in Havana and told Cubans:

> "Openly and unabashedly they are organizing training camps; openly and unabashedly they are building air bases and air strips. Everyone knows who is building the strips and buying planes, that mercenaries are recruiting troops. They even have the cynicism to publish photographs.
>
> Cuba is not located in Africa or on the planet Mars; Cuba is in this hemisphere. Our air space is being violated constantly by planes which do not come from Venus, Africa, or the South Pole, but from this continent. As proof we need only remember that while there is talk of security, our country is kept under constant watch by planes based on this continent, from the United States to Guatemala. Without respect for international law, not only are they openly recruiting weapons but they constantly violate our air space, our jurisdictional waters. With planes and ships they bring explosives here which cost the lives of children, women, and workers, cruelly killed with no other goal than to soften our people. That is the word they use.
>
> With terrorism and bombs they have killed women and children, they have cowardly attacked workers when they leave work, thus they are trying to create counterrevolutionary bands.
>
> What is really offensive to our country and a flagrant violation of international law is that all these activities are directly manipulated and directed from the United States by Central Intelligence Agency agents. That is to say, from there are manipulated the strings of all the conspiracies which kill children and workers, and which cruelly and inhumanely blind lives. It is truly painful that the puppets who are playing into their hands are unaware of the strategy of the Central Intelligence Agency."

Castro wasn't the only one aware of what was coming. Within days of the launch, even the Soviets knew the precise date of the invasion, and broadcasts over Radio Moscow predicted that an operation would begin within a week, with the United States "using paid criminals."[30] KGB agents Osvaldo Sánchez Cabrera and "Aragon" kept Castro fully informed and up to date, while British Ambassador David Ormsby-Gore spoke plainly that British intelligence suggested the Cuban population mostly stood behind Castro and that there was no likelihood of either mass defections or the gathering of a sizeable internal revolution. The Cuban intelligence network was hard at work as well, and the U.S. could barely have made it easier for them, given the loose-

---

[30] Reference.com, The Bay of Pigs Invasion - www.reference.com/browser/Bay+of+Pigs+Invasion.htm

talking exiles operating in Guatemalan bases.

Nevertheless, an armed force of approximately 1,400 Cuban exiles was assembled and sent to train in Petahuleu on the west coast of Guatemala. This corps of Cuban freedom fighters was best known as Brigade 2506, named for the enlistment number of a comrade who died during the training, and it also fell under the moniker of the Cuban Expeditionary Force. On April 14, 1961, they would be carried by six ships from Puerto Cabezas on the coast of Nicaragua to the southern coast of Cuba, operating with the fervent support of Nicaraguan president Luis Somoza, a pro-American leader who urged the soldiers to return with hairs from Castro's beard. A unit of 1,400 would not be considered a major force by modern standards, but it was hoped that disaffected Cubans would join in as the invasion progressed. After all, Castro had overthrown Batista by landing a force of just 81 men, only 11 of whom survived the beginning of the fighting. Those 11 were able to hide in the mountains and cultivate the necessary public sentiment for a coup. The critical difference with the Bay of Pigs invasion was that the altered landing site for the exile force had already rendered such a path logistically difficult even before the fighting started.

As the projected invasion drew near, a tobacco warehouse in Cuba was burned to the ground at a loss of 12 million pesos, and three bombs exploded in and around Havana, with another detonating in Santa Clara. A week later, the U.S. held maneuvers in the Caribbean as a demonstration to Latin American governments and military officials, involving five naval units and a Marine infantry battalion. Incursions into Cuban airspace also increased noticeably. Government factions in Costa Rica and Honduras protested the movement of American-sponsored planes from their borders, and the Workers Party of Guatemala denounced the planned invasion initiated from their shores. One month before the launch, a refinery in Santiago de Cuba was attacked by 50-caliber machine gun fire.

March 16, 1961 was yet another day that made it more difficult for Kennedy to back out of the invasion. He felt an obligation to go forward, but he experienced considerable reluctance in doing so at the same time. When author/historian Arthur Schlesinger asked Kennedy what he thought about the "damned invasion," the president responded that he thought of it "as little as possible."[31] In an April 4th meeting with more than 10 advisors, Senator Fulbright was invited to voice his objections, but all voted to go ahead with the operation, with Dean Rusk being the only non-committal member of the Cabinet. Schlesinger was also invited to outline his concerns, and he opined to Kennedy that the attacking force was too small and could not take control of the country quickly enough. That, he said, would result in a protracted conflict, in which the United States would be perceived as the villain. The President is said to have responded that he had a 24 hour window in which to call the operation off, and that he would see how things progress up to that point. The very same week, Raul Castro responded to the State Department's "white paper" on the status of Cuba, publicly declaring it as tantamount to an act of war and drawing attention to its similarity with the same sort of document that had been published before the Guatemalan

---

[31] National Security Archives

revolution.

Schlesinger

The CIA provided Kennedy with three plans. The first, the Trinidad plan that was rejected, was based on Eisenhower's preference for a large-scale land and air assault in the harbor of Trinidad, 250 miles southeast of Havana and very near the Escambray Mountains. The second plan targeted the northeast coast, which would have placed it in greater proximity to Guantanamo and farther from Havana. The third, to which Kennedy had already expressed a liking, was known as the Zapata plan, which required a landing in a remote, swampy area far from international eyes about 125 miles southeast of Havana: the Bay of Pigs. However, the Bay of Pigs was more than 80 miles away from the Escambray Mountains, making an escape there all but impossible if things went wrong.

A map of the Bay of Pigs region with Trinidad at bottom right and the Escambray Mountains in brown.

In short order, Kennedy ordered a series of modifications to the Zapata plan that would make it appear more guerilla-oriented. Meanwhile, the CIA rounded up every leader of importance in the anti-Castro movement, and met with them at the Skyways Hotel in Miami to achieve unanimity about the plan before proceeding. With the launch date so near, CIA patience was running out for the Cuban exile leadership, and those assembled were told to finalize a committee in short order or the project would be abandoned. The message was delivered in terse, colorful language, and the request had the necessary compliance within three days. A month later, Artime would write his "political testament" to be left behind in case of his death in battle: "This struggle that we are undertaking may mark a new period in Cuban history; we do not seek to overthrow one more tyranny; we seek to extirpate the roots of an international monster that intends to absorb the free world."[32]

On the 9th of April, a large bomb exploded in the elite business district of El Encanto, and three days later, another explosion would reduce a seven-story business in the same district to rubble. The 9th was of great importance because it was also the date that the Cuban exiles in Guatemala received their orders to move toward launching positions. It would take three days to

---
[32] National Security Archives

reach the ships.

In early April, the CIA prepared the way for a successful expansion of the revolution among internal resistance fighters by preparing arms packs for a theoretical 15,000 men and storing them in ships headed for the landing area. Recoilless rifles, mortars, jeeps and trucks were included in these shipments. Ahead of the invasion, CIA operatives were also sent early for the demolition of bridges and other points of infrastructure in order to make it appear that the larger Cuban population supported the regime's overthrow. Meanwhile, teams of divers landed to set up lights in the bay, and two series of raids from the air were designed to eliminate Cuba's air force. Photos of Cuban pilots standing alongside unmarked American planes were circulated to heighten the image of defecting Cubans rescuing their country from a Marxist dictator. These false B-26s, meant to resemble Cuban planes, landed from their missions on April 15th in Miami, badly damaged and with their tanks almost empty. Reconnaissance flights during that week revealed that Cuba was in possession of between 30-36 combat aircraft.

Castro, sensing the uptick in American movement in advance, relocated and camouflaged his best aircraft, leaving decrepit and often unusable craft out in plain sight on his airfields. American-backed bombers would prove unable to hit even these paltry targets, and the Cuban air force remained viable throughout the operation. While Castro knew the invasion plans within the first three hours and sent up planes before dawn, the U.S. government had left the base at Guantanamo largely out of the loop, meaning America military forces that were actually on the island of Cuba were mostly uninformed of the operation.

With only a few days left before the invasion began, CIA Deputy Director of Operations Richard Bissell met with the President, Secretary of State and officials of the National Security Council and the Joint Chiefs of Staff to go over alterations to the Zapata plan. The invasion date was reset for the 17th of April, and two faux air raids would be completed against Cuban installations to make it appear as though they had originated from within the country. The "decoy" landing was planned for Pinar del Rio. By the time of this meeting, the president had still not made a final decision about the invasion, and he was warned that there was no time left for reconsidering the action by a CIA that could not risk cancellation at any cost for fear of losing institutional pride.

Three days before the invasion, Bissell informed the president that the airstrikes could go forward. 16 planes were at the ready, but Kennedy, who wanted a "quiet" operation, believed that such a number was too high-profile and ordered a reduction in the air strength. CIA leadership, in an official reference to Kennedy's overbearing need for secrecy, internally asked, "Even without the air cover, how could a landing of 800 to 1,200 men with tank, heavy machine guns, mortars and recoilless rifles be considered 'quiet?'"[33]

---

[33] CIA Official History of the Bay of Pigs Operation

Regardless, in an arbitrary interpretation of the president's orders, during the early morning hours of April 15, Bissell sent 8 planes into action instead of the full complement, even as he believed that Kennedy had just failed to understand a major aspect of the mission he had just approved. Those 8 planes also happened to be relatively obsolete bombers from the World War II era, with the American markings removed and replaced by markings of the Cuban Fuerza Revolucinario. Furthermore, one diversionary flight was taken over the island to make it appear as though it was a defection to the U.S. that had taken Cuban fire from the ground as it went. The two-seat B-26 was captained by Mario Zuniga, and before taking off from a Nicaraguan airfield, the engine cowling was removed, riddled with bullets and reinstalled. Zuniga flew over the Pina del Rio region in western Cuba, then reset his course to Key West, Florida to the northeast. Once on American (and presumably Cuban) radar, he issued a false Mayday call and landed in Florida. The CIA records of this action do not, understandably, match the Cuban account, but CIA preparation for the diversion required that "pilot and aircraft were to be reamed, steamed, dry-cleaned, sterilized and sanitized...to appear that a legitimate defection...had occurred."[34]

Ultimately, the bombing raid (code-named Operation Puma) targeted three locations in an effort to reduce or eliminate Castro's air power, and Castro himself witnessed the attack on Libertad from General Staff Headquarters, where he was attending a meeting. However, while initial reports suggested that approximately "50% were destroyed at Camp Libertad, 75% to 80% at San Antonio de los Banos, and five planes destroyed at Santiago de Cuba"[35], all of these reports grossly overestimated the damage inflicted. The raids were to have gone through 48 hours of consistent attacks to entirely eliminate the Cuban Air Force, but they fell well short of that mark; not only did the bombers fail to hit much of anything of value, but photos of the planes quickly circulated and offered evidence of American involvement in the raid, despite efforts to conceal American participation. After U-2 photos taken on April 16 indicated that less damage than believed was done, Kennedy canceled the subsequent planned air raid, still hoping to conceal American participation and maintain plausible deniability. The CIA ruefully noted that Kennedy's decision to call off the air strikes after the first wave "had been reached without consulting anyone in the agency."[36]

By the late morning of April 15, just hours after the bombing raid, the Cuban ambassador to the United Nations accused the U.S. of aggression against Cuba. During the emergency session, Adlai Stevenson, the U.S. Ambassador to the United Nations, was unaware of what had transpired and claimed in good faith that America would not intervene in Cuban affairs "under any conditions". Needless to say, he was gravely embarrassed to hear allegations of an invasion come in after stating unequivocally that there was no American intent to invade. Stevenson's humiliation was all the more harsh in light of the fact that he was showing photos of the false diversionary landing (thinking them to be authentic) during the emergency session, where he was

---

[34] CIA Official History of the Bay of Pigs Operation
[35] World History Report: Bay of Pigs Invasion - www.worldhistoryproject.org/1961/4/17/bay-of-pigs-invasion
[36] CIA Official History of the Bay of Pigs Operation

present to answer Cuban accusations on behalf of the American government.

Stevenson wasn't the only one kept out of the loop. As proof of just how far the Kennedy Administration went to deny involvement and maintain secrecy, Secretary of State Dean Rusk also publicly denied any American intention to invade or otherwise intrude in Cuban affairs on April 15, suggesting that "what happens in Cuba is for the Cuban people to decide."[37] Rusk had been lied to by the CIA and was none the wiser. Kennedy, of course, had no excuse and was merely trying to maintain the deception when he stated on April 15, "I have emphasized before that this was a struggle of Cuban patriots against a Cuban dictator. While we could not be expected to hide our sympathies, we made it repeatedly clear that the armed forces of this country would not intervene in any way."

In addition to the embarrassment suffered by senior American officials, the Administration's insistence on secrecy and a policy devoid of overt American support meant that help could not be sent when and where needed if the anti-Castro forces ran into trouble or something went wrong. As the initial bombing raid of April 15 proved, things were not even close to going perfectly, and in fact, the failure of the bombing raid should have come as a surprise to nobody who was being kept informed of the ongoing plans. CIA documents give detailed descriptions of the training Cuban crews received on foreign and domestic bases, at times referring to the entire project as a "comedy of errors." Crews with a significant accumulation of flight hours dropped payloads on top of power plants, tore off parts of wings by flying too close to outcroppings, resorted to emergency landings on beaches, and suffered herniated diaphragms trying to correct disastrous landing approaches. The personal pilot of Guatemala's President Ydigoras "borrowed" a CIA plane and wrecked the landing gear, not on the approved airstrip but on a grass-covered log lying on the personal airstrip at the president's home. Close to the invasion date, the CIA's general view was that there were only "five Cuban pilots of highly technical competence."[38]

For their part, the Cuban pilots and crews were disgruntled over the lack of rank distinction, employing only various colored baseball caps with which to tell each other apart. Segregation between Cuban and American personnel was a sore point, and Cubans often remarked that should the invasion turn out to be a success, they would have to fight all over again with their American comrades to decide once and for all who was in control. A few disillusioned Cuban pilots and crewmen resigned from the program and returned to the States. In a comment tinged with racism, the CIA internally worried about the emotional makeup of the typical Cuban. Other obstacles inhibited progress as well, such as mix-ups with plane markings, and shortages of paint caused five raids to be cancelled due to the absence of Nicaraguan markings.

Chapter 5: April 16-19

"There's an old saying that victory has a hundred fathers and defeat is an orphan...Further

---

[37] www.marxists.org
[38] CIA Official History of the Bay of Pigs Operation

statements, detailed discussions, are not to conceal responsibility because I'm the responsible officer of the Government..." – John F. Kennedy

Even though the CIA had envisioned an operation that primarily relied on airpower, the ground troop landing at Baha Honda in the Pina del Rio province went off as planned on the night of April 16, even though a large gathering of small boats broadcasted the sounds of a major invasion. Four heavy chartered transports (the *Houston*, *Rio Escondido*, *Caribe* and *Atlántico*) were preceded by a unit of frogmen in inflatable boats at the main landing site, but the forces soon encountered the kinds of problems that had long dissuaded military commanders from attempting amphibious landings at night. The *Blagar*, the operation's command ship, landed at Playa Girón (Operation Pluto), accompanied by supply ship *Barbara J.*, which was carrying ordnance, supplies and equipment. However, unloading personnel and equipment at night was delayed by engine problems and damage caused by coral reefs previously thought to be beds of seaweed, and the unloading took so long that the meager Cuban forces that met the landing party were able to contact the country's central forces by radio before being overwhelmed.

With one exile battalion coming ashore at the Playa Girón and the other landing at the Playa Larga beaches, the plan called for the two units to meet in the middle while a smaller group was sent north to secure the town of Jaquey Grande. The exiles hoped to reach support among the native rebels gathered in the Escambray Mountains, but they were unaware that many of the rebels in that region had already been encircled by Castro's forces. In fact, some of them had already been executed by the time of the invasion's launch, and Castro's police had already begun the process of rounding up suspected rebels. The month of April would see an untold number of Cubans executed and hundreds of thousands imprisoned.

With their air force intact as a result of the failed and canceled air raids, Cuban planes reached the landing point well before the "umbrella" of American fighters, which arrived one hour behind schedule due to a miscalculation of time zones, yet another major gaffe in the timing of the operation. Thus, by daybreak, the rebels' ships were attacked from the air by Sea Furies, T-33s and B-26s. The older prop-propelled T-33 still possessed superior speed, and there was no American presence in the air to stop it. The Cuban planes attacked while the unloading of troops was still incomplete, and Cuban pilot Enrique Carreras Rojas sank the invasion force command vessel *Maropa*. The *Houston* was so severely damaged by rocket fire that the captain intentionally beached her two hours later. 180 survivors who had not yet embarked eventually reached the shore, but without weaponry or supplies, they were unable to participate in the action. By the time American aircraft arrived, the skies belonged to Castro, and the promised support had utterly failed to materialize. American B-26s managed to sink the Cuban escort ship *El Blaire*, but it was far too little and too late. With American involvement becoming more and more obvious, Rusk pressured Kennedy to call off implementation of any subsequent air strikes.

A Cuban Hawker Sea Fury FB.11 fighter on display at the Playa Giron Museum.

Without help from the air, and with damaged ships, the rebels that had landed found themselves immediately unable to maintain a supply line, and as a result, "the logistics broke down"[39]. The shore parties realized at once that they were in serious trouble. At a time when they were supposed to be on the move and consolidating gains, they instead found themselves in a protracted battle of tanks against heavy Soviet equipment, The land battle was described as "bloody," fought with a Russian tactic that was not advantageous to guerilla warfare, with large numbers of men on foot against heavy armor. Two hours later, 177 paratroopers landed on Horquita, a town inland from the Playa Larga (code-named Operation Falcon), but bad weather and various coordination failures inhibited a raid on Puerto Cabezas.

By the afternoon of April 17th, Castro himself seems to have taken charge of the defense against the landing, and over the next 72 hours, the exile landing party was pounded by 12 mm. Howitzers, 22 mm. cannon, and heavy tank fire. Castro was able to direct the actual fighting so far from Havana due to the presence of his commanders, Jose Ramon Fernandez, and the Hispano-Soviet Francisco Ciutat de Miguel. Around the same time, a letter to Kennedy arrived from Khrushchev informing the president that the world knew what was happening and that disguising the action so clumsily was absurd. He reminded the American president that "it is not too late to avoid the irreparable."[40]

By April 18th, the second day of the invasion, the only air action of the day saw six B-26s

---

[39] Studyworld.com - 20th Century: The Bay of Pigs Invasion - www.studyworld.com/Bay-of-Pigs-Invasion.htm
[40] www.marxist.org

attack Cuban ground forces with bombs, napalm and rocket fire. While this caused heavy casualties, the rebels still lacked true air superiority without a more forceful or visible American presence. With no hope of escaping to the mountains, the rebels soon found themselves outnumbered nearly 20-1 by Castro's forces, but even as Castro's forces began to beat back the rebels and push them toward the beaches again, Kennedy was insistent in an April 18 communication to Khrushchev that the U.S. had nothing to do with the invasion:

"Dear Chairman:

You are under a serious misapprehension in regard to events in Cuba. For mothers there has been evident and growing resistance to the Castro dictatorship. More than 100,000 refugees have recently fled from Cuba into neighboring countries. Their urgent hops is naturally to assist their fellow Cubans in their struggle for freedom…

These are unmistakable signs that Cubans find intolerable the denial of democratic liberties and the subversion of the 26th of July Movement by an alien-dominated regime. It cannot be surprising that, as resistance within Cuba grows, refugees have been using whatever means are available to return and support their countrymen in the continuing struggle for freedom…

I have previously stated, and I repeat now, that the United States intends no military intervention in Cuba. In the event of any military intervention by outside force we will immediately honor our obligations under the inter-American system to protect this hemisphere against external aggression. While refraining from military intervention in Cuba, the people of the United States do not conceal their admiration for Cuban patriots who wish to see a democratic system in an independent Cuba. The United States government can take no action to stifle the spirit of liberty…"

During the 19th, the invading ground troops were eventually forced back to the beaches. The final air attack took place that day, with crews from the CIA and the Alabama National Guard. Two were shot down, and four Americans were killed. Off the beach, a hasty evacuation attempt was made when Admiral Robert Dennison deployed several unmarked U.S. Navy boats, defended from the air by six unmarked F3H Demon fighters from the carrier USS *Independence*. Although a number of retreating exiles were rescued from the beach, the majority never reached the shore, despite a U.S. destroyer firing on the beach batteries to aid the evacuation.

Although Kennedy had expressed support and good intentions for the Cuban exiles, neither president had much to offer in the way of a moral basis for the invasion, or any significant support to be found in international law. Kennedy's sensitivity to this was evident, not only by withdrawing air cover to protect American identity with the invasion but also in his refusal to follow up with full and open military action, which despite Castro's armed numbers would almost certainly have overwhelmed his revolutionary government. After so much of the expert advice from administration officials and leadership of the CIA had gone wrong, nothing could persuade Kennedy to make further advances against Castro. Procedurally, he was in a state of shock over "what he approved and what in reality occurred."[41] Among the mistaken assumptions in the government's strategy was an assumption that the ground on and around the Bay of Pigs was suitable for guerilla warfare, where it was clearly not. Further, the CIA had made unfounded promises to the exiles, guaranteeing that swift and complete "American military support would follow if necessary."[42]

Chapter 6: The Aftermath of the Failed Invasion

"Thanks for Playa Girón. Before the invasion, the revolution was weak. Now it's stronger than ever." – Che Guevara

By the end of the 19th, it was clear that the invasion was a colossal failure. Estimates of Cuban losses have never been definitively published, but it was estimated at the time to be in the thousands. In a more conservative estimate, 114 of the exile army were killed, with many others surrendering. A few fled to the hills, and 36 would later die as prisoners. Although victorious, Castro's forces suffered horrific casualties during the operation. In one air strike alone, a mix of army, militia, police and civilians were caught out in the open causeways of the swamps in civilian buses, with the result of nearly 2,000 dead.

President Kennedy, with a past based in journalism that may have made him less inclined toward cover-ups than others, spoke publicly on April 27 about the failed invasion. Despite an awareness of his involvement in and culpability for the invasion's basic ethics and implementation, his speech was apparently designed to open the incident to investigation, serving as an expression of his general credo regarding the "fourth estate" as well: "No official of my administration, whether his rank is high or low, civilian or military, should interpret my words here tonight as an excuse to censor the news, to stifle dissent, or to withhold from the press and the public the facts they deserve to know."[43]

In the meantime, Castro moved quickly to bring all of those captured to trial for treason, over 1,200 in number despite the fact some were executed before that could be arranged: "Enemies of the revolution were neutralized, arrested, or shot while resisting arrest...unceremoniously rounded up and corralled into any facility available."[44] The remainder of the force was sentenced to 30 years in prison, but after 20 months of negotiations, the exiles were released in exchange for $53 million worth of food and medicine. Before then, however, hundreds of executions took place over the next six months, including those of infiltration team leader Antonio Diaz Pou and

---

[41] Joshua Sandman, p. 313
[42] Joshua Sandman, p. 313
[43] Richard Belzer, "Lamentations and Regrets", Huffington Post
[44] Reference.com - Bay of Pigs Invasion

Raimondo E. Lopez. Student leaders Virgilio Campaneria and Alberto Topia were also executed, along with many of their followers.

Kennedy addressing released members of Brigade 2506 in December 1962.

Despite the lack of collaboration between the two administrations, Kennedy sent for Eisenhower immediately following the failed invasion. The former president is said to have asked Kennedy why air cover had been withdrawn, and Kennedy responded by expressing fear that the Soviets would "make trouble"[45] in Berlin. Eisenhower countered, "That is exactly the opposite of what would really happen."[46] Eisenhower also prophetically told the president that

---
[45] Joshua Sandman, p. 311

"the failure of the Bay of Pigs will embolden the Soviets to do something that they would otherwise not do."

Bay of Pigs memorial in the Little Havana section of Miami.

CIA declassifications are an important commentary in the now largely extant review of the Bay of Pigs invasion, in part because an investigation was commissioned by the President himself on April 22, 1961. Maxwell Taylor headed the commission with the peripheral assistance of Robert Kennedy, Admiral Arleigh Burke and Director Allen Dulles. Numerous attempts were made to declassify the Maxwell Taylor report in previous years, but permission was required from the

---

[46] Joshua Sandman, p. 312

Pentagon, the CIA and other government agencies. Brief, heavily censored excerpts emerged throughout the first decade following the invasion, but the bulk has only recently come to light and is still censored in some documents. When the first major sections of the commission were released in 1999, the reason cited for the delay was that the Pentagon had lost the report. However, the full transcript and audio file is still held by the JFK Library.

Taylor

The resulting report amounts to what is referred to by an officer of the National Security Administration as a "scathing document."[47] According to the Newsweek magazine staff, it is "the most brutally frank and honest government document ever written."[48] With much blame to go around, not all the faulty planning lay with the Kennedy Administration, and the alterations to the plan (for which the president is blamed), in addition to the cancellation of two days of airstrikes, were not all discovered until a later time. It is generally agreed that had the two days of airstrikes before the landing been restored, Cuba's air power could have been largely wiped out. Kennedy, not fully realizing what the CIA was about, rejected a plan that might have worked more successfully, that of landing at Trinidad, a generally anti-communist community with a harbor suitably constructed for the purpose. Whatever revolution he hoped would be

---
[47] National Security Archives
[48] National Security Archives

sparked on the island had its best chance in Trinidad, and even in the event of a failed landing, the exile force might have been given access to escape routes. Once again, however, part of Kennedy's misunderstanding can be placed at the feet of the previous administration. Throughout Eisenhower's tenure, he continually rejected "clear evidence of Castro's political and military strength, which was available from British and State Department intelligence, and even newspaper stories."[49]

The failure of the Bay of Pigs, in addition to casting a pall over the presidency in the immediate aftermath, highlighted the heightened powers of an agency that had covered itself in glory only a few years back in Guatemala and Iran. The tendency for an agency such as the CIA to rely too literally on precedent, even from successful operations, was evident in the approach to Cuba, because the Cuban situation bore too few similarities to the previous era. In fact, not only was the available information concerning public opinion in Cuba suppressed within the CIA and withheld from the President, but it was in many cases not even requested. The CIA understood that without significant American involvement, "there was little hope that the amateurish Cuban underground might succeed on its own."[50] Although disenchantment with Castro was present among the Cubans, and the CIA sensed, perhaps correctly, that anti-Castro sentiments were somewhat on the increase, it was an irrational assumption to rely upon the model of the Guatemalan revolution. Unlike that nation, Castro had assembled an armed force of approximately 200,000 and made numerous other preparations for an American attack. It was equally irrational to think that American involvement could be hidden in any sense.

At the same time, the CIA was aware of its advantage over the White House in 1961. President Kennedy had been in office for only a few months when he was suddenly handed a pre-arranged plan and was asked only for his rubber-stamp approval. He was unable to consider the issue and formulate a policy, only able to accept or reject this inheritance from the Eisenhower version of the CIA. The agency pressed Kennedy hard on the matter, "displaying typical organizational imperialism."[51] Well before the invasion, the CIA records quote from the top strata: "Our second concept (1,500-3,000 man force to secure a beach with airstrip) is also now seen to be unachievable, except as a joint Agency/DOD (Department of Defense) action."[52] This can only be taken to mean that the Department of Defense, in an overt American military offensive, would have been required for the overthrow of Castro, not a small, covert action requiring numerous points of coordination and employing lightly armed Cuban exiles. Most importantly, however, this agency view was never presented to the President, and as in other cases, he proceeded with either faulty or incomplete counsel.

It was also the CIA that prized secrecy to the point that the necessary American forces could

---

[49] Joshua H. Sandman, "Analyzing Foreign Policy Crisis Situations: The Bay of Pigs", in *Presidential Studies Quarterly*, Vol. 16 No. 2, Spring 1986, p. 311
[50] Lucien S. Vandenbroucke, "Anatomy of a Failure: The Decision to Land at the Bay of Pigs", in *Political Science Quarterly*, Vol. 99 No. 3, Autumn, 1984, p. 472
[51] Lucien S. Vandenbroucke, p. 472
[52] CIA Official History of the Bay of Pigs Operation

not be brought to bear on the situation. Secrecy, among the CIA's most prized possessions, eliminated a host of dissenters, making formulation of the plan much easier, and once the President could be pressured into approving the plan, "the CIA enjoyed a prized bureaucratic resource - control of information."[53] To Kennedy's misfortune, one of those dissenters cut out from the plan was the State Department's Bureau of Intelligence and Research, an agency that could have easily provided a more realistic picture of Cuban psychology in planning for an invasion requiring indigenous participation. Furthermore, the CIA never provided written documents to the Joint Chiefs of Staff, and in the case of every White House meeting, agency officials collected the documents at the end, including those given to the President. Over the few weeks in which Kennedy could sift through the available information, the agency presented only those reports to the White House it wanted to release, and it backpedaled on many of the plan's deficiencies. Never mentioned were reports on the status of Castro's reinforcements, or the innumerable "pessimistic reports from independent observers."[54]

In other circumstances, the Pentagon could have served as a deterrent to the CIA's unbridled influence, but with the limited scope of the Cuban operation, the mainstream military was entirely peripheral and had only been asked to render advice. With little at stake for the military's reputation, the branches all went along as well, and with such an incomplete portfolio, Kennedy began to make alterations without understanding that he was crippling major aspects of the operation, including reducing air power and later canceling strikes. The CIA knew that the exiles didn't have the necessary air power, but it did not impress upon the President the importance of full air cover for fear that he would cancel the operation altogether, project a weak appearance internationally, and produce a large mass of disgruntled Cuban exiles who trained under the assumption that the operation would be launched in the near future.

It was certainly in the CIA's best self-interest to maintain its lofty status as a heroic American agency, and to have the rug pulled out from under it by the White House would have resulted in a humiliation from which it could take years to recover. In the aftermath of the failed invasion, Allen Dulles (Director of the CIA), Charles Cabell (Deputy Director) and Richard Bissell (Deputy Director of Operations) were all forced to resign. The official CIA report, released years later, would state that "what happened in the air not only *could,* but *did* determine the fate of the US government's anti-Castro program."[55]

In reference to the Bay of Pigs fiasco, it is nearly unanimous that the White House, CIA, State Department and armed forces produced, through this epic institutional debacle, that "rarest of all things - a perfect failure."[56] However, while the Bay of Pigs was unquestionably an unmitigated disaster, it would have a profound effect on how Kennedy went about mulling his options during the Cuban Missile Crisis. The president believed he had been all but played by the CIA and

---

[53] Lucien S. Vandenbroucke, p. 474
[54] Lucien S. Vandenbroucke, p. 476
[55] CIA Official History of the Bay of Pigs Operation
[56] Luis E. Rumbaut and Rubén G. Rumbaut, "Survivor: Cuba: The Cuban Revolution at 50", in *Latin American Perspectives*, Vol. 36 No. 1, January 2009

boxed into a military option in 1961, and he wasn't about to let that happen again. As he put it to a friend in the wake of the Bay of Pigs fiasco, "The first advice I'm going to give my successor is to watch the generals and to avoid feeling that because they were military men their opinions on military matters were worth a damn."

Chapter 7: Kennedy and Khrushchev Meet at Vienna

Just months into his Presidency, Kennedy was severely embarrassed. Hailed as a foreign policy expert with military experience during the campaign, Kennedy's ability to conduct American foreign policy was now firmly in question, and it would be eagerly put to the test by Khrushchev. Moreover, Fidel Castro remained wary of a U.S. invasion, which would have serious implications for another crisis a year and a half later. And as if the news couldn't get worse for the young president, April 1961 also witnessed the first manned space flight by Soviet cosmonaut Yuri Gagarin, handing the Soviets another major propaganda victory.

However, all of these embarrassments stiffened Kennedy's resolve ahead of the Vienna Summit on June 3, 1961, and as a result, Kennedy had no intention of making any concessions. American presidents had experienced such trouble with Soviet leaders before, entering with refined European-style sensibilities to meet well-informed but highly focused non-diplomats with a street thug style of expression by comparison. In this case, Kennedy could not have faced a more experienced counterpart, as Khrushchev became Soviet premier in 1958 after five years as First Secretary of the Communist Party. He was central to the Soviet desire to possess Germany, and he had learned at the feet of Stalin during the blockade of Berlin. Four years before meeting Kennedy, Khrushchev had tangled with Nixon, a somewhat pugnacious man himself, and he had delivered the "we will bury you" speech, widely misinterpreted as the threat of a nuclear strike. Such a misinterpretation did not help Western instincts during the upcoming missile crisis.

Khrushchev and Kennedy meet at Vienna

In their first and only face-to-face meeting (and the last meeting between a Soviet leader and an American president until the Nixon Administration), neither Kennedy nor Khrushchev were in a mood to compromise. They were at loggerheads over a four-power treaty to settle the question of the two Germanys and Berlin, and over an atmospheric test-ban treaty. Both men seemingly left the Summit empty handed, but the Americans realized immediately that the summit meeting was a catastrophe. Elder statesmen had warned the Kennedy Administration that Khrushchev was an unpredictable bully, at least in his behavior, and it was fervently recommended that the president allow lower-level diplomats to manage the issues at hand with their Soviet counterparts. Dean Rusk, Secretary of State, was far more familiar with the Khrushchev style of close in-fighting and asked, "Is it wise to gamble too heavily? Are not these two men who should be kept apart until others have found a sure meeting ground of accommodation between them?" Kennedy, however, went ahead, confident in his Ivy League education, his extensive study on communism and his natural eloquence, none of which served him well in a meeting with Khrushchev.

According to diplomats in attendance, Kennedy was "pummeled by the Soviet leader…despite his eloquence, Kennedy was no match as a sparring partner." On the first morning of the first day, Kennedy was endlessly lectured on American hypocrisy in matters of foreign policy, and the ways in which America had lost her glory after first standing up to the British. Kennedy could hardly get a word in against Khrushchev, and he complained upon exiting the chamber that he'd been treated like "a little boy." Kennedy later told his brother Bobby that it was "like dealing with Dad. All give and no take."

The American contingent was shocked that Kennedy had accepted such abuse, and Khrushchev left Vienna in a state of elation, decrying the American as "inexperienced, even immature". Among the parting shots of the Vienna debacle was a declaration by Khrushchev that he was going to sign the treaty, and that it was up to America to decide whether it wanted to have a war over it. Entering the summit, Kennedy had failed to realize that any initial summit with Khrushchev was not, for the Soviets, primarily intended for the exchange of information or search for common ground but to establish a pecking order and to set a standard of intimidation for continual use in the future.

Aware of what had happened over the two days, Kennedy left Vienna worried. In particular, he was understandably concerned about what kind of moves the Soviet premier might make if he believed the American leadership had no guts. As Kennedy correctly assumed, Khrushchev would walk away from the summit believing he could trample all over American foreign policy until shown otherwise.

Chapter 8: Khrushchev Makes a Decision

Khrushchev came away from the meeting still thinking he could push the young president around, but the failure once again to settle the question of Berlin put Khrushchev in a difficult situation. East Germany was pushing for a solution to the problem of an enclave of freedom within its borders. West Berlin was a haven for highly-educated East Germans who wanted freedom and a better life in the West, and this "brain drain" was threatening the survival of the East German economy. In order to stop this, access to the West through West Berlin had to be cut off, so in August 1961 Khrushchev authorized East German leader Walter Ulbricht to begin construction of what would become known as the Berlin Wall. The wall, begun on August 13, would eventually surround the city, in spite of global condemnation, and the Berlin Wall itself would become the symbol for Communist repression in the Eastern Bloc. It also ended Khrushchev's attempts to conclude a peace treaty among the Four Powers (the Soviet Union, the U.S., the U.K., and France) and the two German states.

In the wake of the Berlin Wall's construction, however, Khrushchev's meager view of Kennedy seemed to be playing out as expected, since no Soviet action drew an American response worth any bother. When the Berlin Wall went up, Kennedy didn't contest it, accepting that it was a better alternative than war. Thus, when the Cuba missile project was drawn up, Khrushchev described it as "throwing a hedgehog at Uncle Sam's pants." Even with an incursion into territories a few miles off American coasts, it was Khrushchev's belief that Kennedy would "fuss, fuss some more," then retreat and accept.

Many factors and a troublesome historical timeline for America certainly contributed to the Soviet confidence in executing such a bold maneuver. For one thing, installing missiles in Cuba had also been made possible by events in Cuba itself and elsewhere. Castro's revolution had overthrown the Cuban dictator Batista the very same year that American Jupiter missiles began to be placed in Turkey and Italy. The final placement of those missiles in Turkey and Italy would take place in April 1962, and they had been spurred in part by the fact that the West (along with much of the world) fell for Khrushchev's bogus proclamation of the Soviets' superiority in ICBMs. Kennedy professed his intent to work at reducing the gap when he unknowingly already held the advantage, but his subsequent warnings to the Soviets that the United States would not be challenged in the Western Hemisphere were weakened by his announcement that while surface-to-surface missiles would not be allowed in Cuba, surface-to-air missiles (SAMs) would be permitted as defensive weapons. Through this, the Soviets had both an opening to bring in one type of weapon, and a camouflaged excuse to smuggle in another.

A Jupiter missile

Although Kennedy was unaware of it, it was the Soviets who were behind in the missile gap. For them, leveling the nuclear playing field was a priority, and to put nuclear weapons in

America's backyard was perfectly logical, just as the reverse was true with American missiles standing in Turkey and Italy being aimed at Moscow. While the decision to install missiles in Cuba required a hard-nosed personality and obvious fortitude, those characteristics definitely fit the 67 year old Khrushchev to a tee. Furthermore, he was not making this maneuver without a personal awareness of his foe; Khrushchev carried a deplorably low opinion of the American president because he had in every way mauled the younger man at the Vienna summit. Considering the rapidity by which events unfolded during the years of 1960 to 1962, all the available options on the table and a myriad of possible outcomes, many of them gloomy ones, it may have been expected by serious diplomats on both sides that the less experienced, theory-minded American administration would in some way buckle under the pressure.

Moreover, several advantages beyond the obvious played in favor of Khrushchev. By installing missiles in Cuba, he could pay the U.S. back for their installations in Italy and Turkey, and he could further test the resolve of the United States and its young president, who he believed could be "intimidated and blackmailed." Finally, Khrushchev believed that such installations, whether resisted or not, could ultimately become bargaining chips for future actions in Europe.

The Soviets thought all of this would seemingly be made easier by Castro's willingness to affiliate with them. However, even given Castro's utter rejection of the U.S., immediate problems developed with Cuban-Soviet relations as well. Castro's ample ego could not tolerate being a Soviet puppet, and it was severely bruised when his application to join the literal Soviet bloc was denied. Subsequent financial assistance from the Soviets was insufficient and less than promised. Further, he did not ask for the weaponry foisted on Cuba by the Soviet government, but that might have still been no big deal if there weren't Soviet fingers on the buttons. Castro figured that any weapons installed in Cuba could be used at his own discretion. Had he received them along with the control to use them, minus the Soviet military contingent and their in-house chain of launch authorization, it might have been another matter, but the Soviets realized far in advance the danger of allowing a newly-emerged freedom fighter to carry out a nuclear attack on the U.S. Khrushchev and his administration were also unsettled by the fact that communism in Cuba was not developing in the orthodox way and was overseen by a non-Soviet without preeminence of the Communist Party. In personal terms, Castro's greatest difficulty with the missile crisis was that it had not been of his making, and he had never been consulted nor put in command, which he found to be personally offensive.

Throughout 1962, Soviet military officers accompanied trade groups to Cuba to scout and choose secret military installations in which to place Soviet missiles. When one Soviet delegation to Cuba arrived in Havana on May 29, 1962, it included Marshal S. Biryuzov, Commander of Strategic Rocket Forces. The meeting was successfully held in confidence, and a little more than a month later, Fidel's brother Raul arrived in Moscow. By September, the Soviet freighter *Omsk* had arrived in Cuba with the first shipment of ICBMs, and the second ship to arrive, on September 15, was the *Polatavia*, also a freighter, carrying a shipment of medium range ballistic missiles. By the 20th of October, 20-30 ships were en route to Havana, and it was estimated that the number of missiles already in Cuba numbered around 40.

Soviet archives actually contest some of these figures (which appeared in later CIA reports), claiming that "85 Soviet ships had made 180 trips to Cuba before the U.S. established a blockade." These archives provide a key to the extreme secrecy which brought the weapons under the very noses of the U.S., well-prepared with numerous side-deceptions. Even en route to Cuba, "Soviet soldiers and officers did not know their destinations…units would board tropics-bound ships with all their equipment and supplies including winter coats and woolen boots…soldiers were prohibited to come upstairs…bodies of dead were dropped overboard." In a further confirmation of the crisis timeline, Soviet records state (in contrast to CIA briefings) that "the first missile unit led by I.S. Sidirov was declared operational on October 20, with two hours and thirty minutes required for firing the missile," considerably less than intelligence estimates about the time needed to launch. The Soviet inventory was officially listed as including 60 warheads for R-12 and R-14 ballistic missiles, 12 warheads for Luna short-range missiles, 80 warheads for cruise missiles, 6 aircraft-based nuclear bombs, 4 sea-based naval mines, and a projected operation and defensive set of personnel numbering over 40,000.

Regardless of the actual numbers, what is clear is that while working secretly under the codename Operation Anadyr, a name that itself was intended to deceive the Americans into believing it concerned the Bering Sea a hemisphere away, the Soviets went about secretly transporting nuclear missiles and placing them in Cuba. In August, American intelligence exposed the existence of Soviet aircraft in Cuba, as well as anti-aircraft batteries, but even though they realized that some of the Soviet ships headed to Cuba could carry missiles, there would be no definitive intelligence about it until American spy planes found already operational missile sites in October.

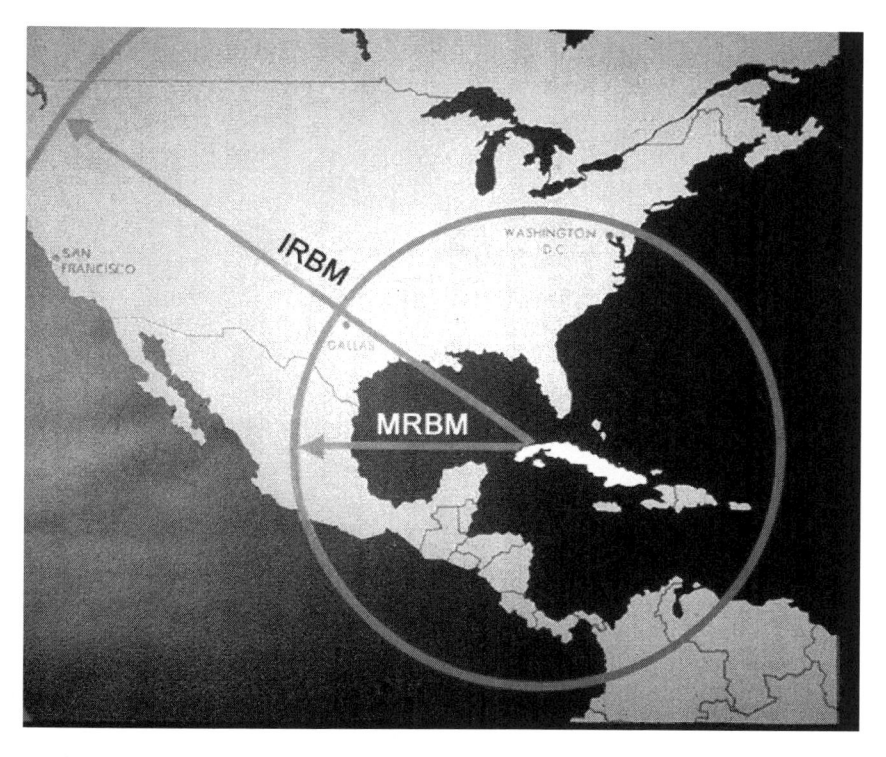

A CIA map indicating the range of medium and intermediate range ballistic missiles from Cuba.

Chapter 9: U-2s Over Cuba

An American spy plane photograph of a nuclear missile site on Cuba. The picture shows transporters and tents where fueling and maintenance of the missiles could be done.

On October 7, 1962, Cuban officer Osvaldo Dorticós hinted at what was going on when he told the U.N. General Assembly, "If ... we are attacked, we will defend ourselves. I repeat, we have sufficient means with which to defend ourselves; we have indeed our inevitable weapons, the weapons, which we would have preferred not to acquire, and which we do not wish to employ." But the definitive proof would not come until a week later.

Despite the embarrassment of having Gary Powers shot down in 1960, the U-2 spy plane was a reconnaissance marvel that fully functioned at an altitude of 70,000 feet or higher. For purposes of reconnaissance over Cuba, it was ideal, and numerous classified missions were flown out of Laughlin Air Force Base in Texas. In fact, U-2 planes might have discovered evidence of Soviet missile sites earlier but for the fact that Kennedy was worried about Soviet SAMs already being present on Cuba. Thus, the Administration initially wanted to conduct surveillance of Cuba with satellites.

An original U-2 spy plane

Near the end of September, it was discovered that a Soviet ship was carrying crates big enough to carry Soviet bombers, and furthermore, photos showed that SAMs on Cuba were arranged in a similar fashion as those that protected nuclear missile sites back in the Soviet Union. Thus, on Sunday, October 14, Major Richard Heyser of the 4080th Strategic Reconnaissance Command climbed into a U-2 plane at Edwards Air Force Base in California for a mission dubbed BRASS KNOB, The mission would take several hours to reach and fly across Cuba, and he would only be above Cuba for a matter of minutes on his way to a landing in Florida after about 7 hours. The intelligence network provided detailed coordinates for the flight, mostly through the efforts of a double spy for the U.S. and U.K. named Colonel Oleg Penkovsky, who was later arrested by the KGB and executed.

Heyser's flight was afforded by the first clear skies in two weeks, but as historian Chris Pocock noted in *50 Years of the U-2: The Complete Illustrated History of the 'Dragon Lady'*, it was a mission fraught with risk: "He met the sun over the Gulf of Mexico, and flew over the Yucatan Channel before turning north to penetrate denied territory. The weather was roughly as forecast: 25% cloud cover. He was flying the maximum altitude profile, and by this time the U-2F had reached 72,500 feet. There was no contrail. Heyser switched on the camera and did his stuff. He was over the island for less than seven minutes, but his potential exposure to the two SAM sites was over 12 minutes. Heyser had been briefed to scan the driftsight for Cuban fighters or, worse still. an SA-2 heading his way. If so, he was briefed to turn sharply towards it, and then away from it, in an S-pattern that would hopefully break the missile radar's lock. But there was no opposition from Cuba's air defenses. Heyser coasted-out and headed for McCoy AFB, Florida. He landed there at 0920 EST after exactly seven hours in the air."

Kennedy meets with Heyser (left) after his reconnaissance flight.

The photography run of the U-2 has been likened to the same set of principles as a bombing run, in which the "platform" must remain steady as possible. Thus, Major Heyser hovered around what was called "coffin corner" at 75,000 feet, "where the air was so thin it could barely support the weight of the plane." Flying directly over San Cristobal, Heyser was able to take 3,000 frames in a span of seven to twelve minutes, ultimately acquiring clear evidence that Soviet SS-4 intermediate range nuclear missiles were already present, that SS-2 surface to air missile installations were under construction, and in a typical Soviet pattern, surrounding the surface to surface installations. Heyser would later note that he was deathly concerned about the results of his mission, and that it might be what touched off nuclear war. As he explained in an interview, "I kind of felt like I was going to be looked at as the one who started the whole thing. I wasn't anxious to have that reputation."

Chapter 10: Kennedy Makes a Decision and a Speech

Following an analysis at the National Photographic Intelligence Center on October 15, the Central Intelligence Agency summarized its findings in a report to the president about what the pictures showed: "We estimate that the MRBMs can be fired in eight hours or less after a decision to launch…after the sites are completed, and missiles are on launcher, a state of readiness of five hours may be maintained…both systems are believed to be provided with two missiles per launcher, providing a re-fire capability from each launcher after about four to six additional hours."

Once Kennedy was informed, he assembled a team of advisors that later became known as the "EXCOMM" (Executive Committee of the National Security Council), and they began deliberating over a response. Records revealed in the late 1990s shed some light on Kennedy's general state of mind at the time; and they indicate Kennedy was in a condition of "personal belligerence – a condition sparked largely by anger at what he perceived to be Soviet attempts to deceive him." Rather than finding a kindred spirit in U.S. Ambassador to the United Nations Adlai Stevenson, who recommended a negotiated resolution, Kennedy was originally fixated on an airstrike against the Cuban installations and rejected the Ambassador out of hand. It is noted, however, that his "initial hostility gave way…to a more flexible position," according to historian Arthur Schlesinger, who further observed that the shift occurred very rapidly. Kennedy's initial reaction may have played into a number of other embarrassments, the first of which had begun in the Vienna summit, and it might have tapped into some sense of ill-preparedness for the crisis now at hand.

Kennedy and Secretary of Defense Robert McNamara during an EXCOMM meeting.

After all the analysis from the U-2 photos was made available, EXCOMM and the others involved in crafting a response spent several days deliberating the options, several of which were wildly different than the others. Upon hearing the news and attempting to generate a proper response, some urged using diplomacy to find a resolution, while others insisted that there need not be a response at all, given that the Soviets' first-strike capability from Cuba still wouldn't protect them in the event of a full-scale nuclear exchange. Conversely, there were those who urged air strikes that would take out the known missile sites if not a full-scale invasion, which would overthrow Castro and seize control of Cuba itself.

Not surprisingly, there was never anything remotely approaching a unanimous opinion on which course to take. For example, Secretary of Defense Robert McNamara turned out to be less hawkish than many others, advising against any sort of surprise attack on Soviet or Cuban forces because of the potential harm to be brought down upon Berlin, farther out of America's reach than Cuba but much closer to the Soviets. McNamara rebuffed military assertions that missiles in Cuba altered the balance of power among the Soviets and Americans, later stating in an interview, "It made no difference ... The military balance wasn't changed. I didn't believe it then, and I don't believe it now."

Dean Acheson, who had served as Secretary of State from 1949-1953, remained a close advisor (though not technically serving on EXCOMM) and recommended a narrow strike against only the missile installations, leaving the bombers and runways alone. However, on October 21st, General Walter Sweeney, Commander-in-Chief of the Tactical Air Command, informed Kennedy that air strikes likely couldn't guarantee a complete removal of the missiles, leaving open the possibility that some could be launched. Acheson would later be quoted in the aftermath of the crisis as saying they had survived through a stroke of "dumb luck," not a ringing endorsement of the president's choices, and probably an unfair assessment all the way around.

Acheson

General Curtis LeMay, who had overseen the Berlin airlift and had gained renown during World War II fame, was expectedly proactive in his recommendation of full-out military attack. Disgusted with Kennedy's habitual desire to avoid war if possible, the General issued a stern warning: "We're just going to gradually drift into war under conditions that are at great disadvantage to us…This is almost as bad as the appeasement of Munich." The JFK archival tapes, which included over 248 hours of meetings and over 17 hours of phone conversations, indicated that clear cliques formed among the advisory panel, and groups of military brass could be heard in the outer halls fretting over the need to urge the president into a full-out attack. Among them was General Shoup: "Somebody's got to keep him from doing the goddam thing piecemeal. That's our problem. Go in there and frig around with the missiles. You're screwed. You go in there and screw around with anything else, and you're screwed." Senator Mike Mansfield argued against piecemeal responses as well, declaring, "There is no such thing as a small military action. The moment we start anything…we have to be prepared to do everything."

LeMay

Adlai Stevenson would eventually be called upon to address the U.N. at the height of the crisis, but within the privacy of deliberations, he urged a general approach of moderation and diplomacy. On the 17th of October, five days before Kennedy's national broadcast announced his decision to the world, Stevenson wrote a letter to the president cautioning that "an attack [on Cuba] would very likely result in Soviet reprisals somewhere – Turkey, Berlin, etc. – it is most important that we have as much of the world with us as possible. To start or risk starting a nuclear war is bound to be divisive at best, and the judgments of history seldom coincide with the tempers of the moment."

    In the end, when the shrinking list of responses had come down to various sorts of military actions, diplomatic forays, saber-rattling and grandstanding for international points, or to simply do nothing at all, the advisor in the room that John F. Kennedy trusted the most was his brother Bobby, the Attorney General. Bobby had long served as a critical advisor to his brother and in this case was a counterweight to the aggressive posturing of military brass. Though he had previously taken aggressive stances in Cuba, Bobby was one of the voices who opposed outright war, and along with the president, the two agreed over vociferous objections by the military men that a naval blockade, softened in title to "quarantine", was the correct path to choose. Clearly, President Kennedy was not nearly as bellicose as others who were part of the deliberations, and this may have been due at least in part to Kennedy possessing a strong humanitarian streak. He seemed baffled at every turn when advisors urged "irretrievable" actions, as if contrasts between the nuclear age and conventional warfare had not yet occurred to them.

Bobby Kennedy

At the same time, opting to implement a blockade would set up a contest of wills, and Kennedy didn't have a very good track record against Khrushchev when it came to that. Moreover, the stakes were much higher than they were in Vienna, given the fact there were Soviet ships off the coast of the United States. But even with the stakes raised and a state of high tension pervading the Administration, with many thinking that nuclear war was inevitable, Kennedy was about to draw his line in the sand, and Khrushchev was about to learn he was dealing with an entirely different man than the one he met in Vienna.

Whatever lack of direct battle experience held Kennedy back (at least in the opinions of the military brass), the situation was well-geared to his ability to think and plan in detail, and to gauge consequences from actions on either side. Kennedy also realized that Berlin was as important to the equation as Cuba, perhaps more important, and that an airstrike, successful or not, might bring the Soviet Union into Berlin in much the same way as they had appeared in Hungary, with lightning speed and heavy armor. As Kennedy put it, "They, no more than we, can let these things go by without doing something. They can't, after all their statements, permit us to take out their missiles, kill a lot of Russians, and then do nothing. If they don't take action in Cuba, they certainly will in Berlin." At the same time, Kennedy came to the conclusion that if he were to attack the island of Cuba in the next week to ten days, some of the missiles would likely be fired at the mainland before they could be reached. He interjected the question of large city evacuation from the southeastern metropolitan areas but received little support; in fact, the tapes of one meeting recorded a response from an unknown advisor suggesting that cities offered citizens the best protection from radiation.

Kennedy also understood that in this crisis, the Kremlin had the advantage of geographical priorities. In the JFK tapes, the president's take on the situation and its effects on friendly nations was made clear: "Our allies would think of us as trigger-happy cowboys who lost Berlin because we did not have the guts to endure the situation in Cuba. Cuba is 5,000 to 6,000 miles from Europe, and they don't give a damn about it…this is a very satisfactory position from their point of view." What probably killed the idea of an airstrike was Kennedy's view that the Soviets would take Berlin as a counter, some nuclear weapons in Cuba would remain viable, and America would be forced into using their own nukes.

After Kennedy chose the naval blockade by the end of the meetings on October 21, Admiral George Anderson Jr., the Chief of Naval Operations and the one who would be in charge of the blockade, drafted a paper presenting the legal justification for the "quarantine" that relied on the Rio Treaty. It read in part:

> "Latin American participation in the quarantine now involved two Argentine destroyers which were to report to the US Commander South Atlantic at Trinidad on November 9. An Argentine submarine and a Marine battalion with lift were available if required. In addition, two Venezuelan destroyers (Destroyers 'ARV D-

11 Nueva Esparta' and 'ARV D-21 Zulia') and one submarine (Caribe) had reported to COMSOLANT, ready for sea by November 2. The Government of Trinidad and Tobago offered the use of Chaguaramas Naval Base to warships of any OAS nation for the duration of the 'quarantine.' The Dominican Republic had made available one escort ship. Colombia was reported ready to furnish units and had sent military officers to the US to discuss this assistance. The Argentine Air Force informally offered three SA-16 aircraft in addition to forces already committed to the 'quarantine' operation.

This initially was to involve a naval blockade against offensive weapons within the framework of the Organization of American States and the Rio Treaty. Such a blockade might be expanded to cover all types of goods and air transport. The action was to be backed up by surveillance of Cuba. The CNO's scenario was followed closely in later implementing the 'quarantine.'"

Early on October 22, hours before he would inform the world about Soviet missiles in Cuba, President Kennedy phoned former presidents Hoover, Truman and Eisenhower with a briefing, and he also sent the first in a series of letters directly to Nikita Khrushchev. Meanwhile, in Cuba, Castro mobilized the Cuban armed forces and issued a war alert for the whole of Cuba.

Later that night, a solemn President John F. Kennedy addressed the nation in a live television broadcast and reported to the American people that there had been an abrupt change in the unsteady stalemate between the United States and the Soviet Union. Speaking of the threat to the nuclear weapon balance maintained in previous years, Kennedy stated, "For many years, both the Soviet Union and the United States, recognizing this fact, have deployed strategic nuclear weapons with great care, never upsetting the precarious status quo which insured that these weapons would not be used in the absence of some vital challenge." This speech explained the threat to that balance posed by the Soviet missiles on Cuba.

With all of the potential military ramifications involved in the crisis, conducting a broadcast with such transparency seemed unusual even at that time, but speeches to one audience often include messages to other audiences, and that was part of Kennedy's intent. While he informed the American people of his findings, he took the opportunity to speak directly and indirectly to the Soviet government, the Cuban people, and countries of Central and South America as well.

In the statement, Kennedy cited "unmistakable evidence" of multiple missile silos and airbases in a state of mid-construction on the island of Cuba, and he asserted his assumption, based on U-2 spy plane surveillance conducted over the island on a continual basis, that a Soviet presence in Cuba was intended to "provide a nuclear strike capability against the Western Hemisphere." Providing a surprising amount of detail, he broke the photographed installations into two basic groups, the first for launching or flying (via bombers only then being taken out of their crates after being delivered by Soviet ships) medium range ballistic surface-to-surface missiles, each capable of "carrying a nuclear warhead for a distance of over one thousand nautical miles." Kennedy spelled out the ramifications in terms of geography – that the ability to strike at such a distance included targets such as Washington, D.C., any major city in the Southwestern United States, Cape Canaveral, Mexico City, the Panama Canal, and most targets in countries of Central America and the Caribbean. The other type of installation, he said, was "designed for intermediate range ballistic missiles capable of traveling twice as far." His inference was that any major city in the entire Western Hemisphere would fit inside such a geographical range, and he specifically cited Hudson Bay in Canada and Lima, Peru.

The address, which lasted approximately 18 minutes, went on to enumerate the violations constituted by the Soviet action, including those of his own warnings delivered in that year, the Rio Pact of 1947 (specifically articles 6 and 8), the Joint Resolution of the 87th Congress, and the Charter of the United Nations. Following a summation of the action's illegal basis, Kennedy proceeded to itemize recent verbal and written communications from the Soviet government and its Ambassador to the United States, Alexander Dobrynin, quoting each statement and policy position in detail before labeling each to be patently false. The president was careful to include the watchword of American security, "clear and present danger," to legalize his own response and future responses.

Kennedy speaking to the country about the Cuban Missile Crisis

At this point in time, the world was not yet two decades away from the first use of atomic weapons, and the specter of their further use, or of an all-out nuclear war, was that era's international nightmare. Kennedy was more than aware of this when he reiterated his position that "we will not prematurely or unnecessarily risk the cause of worldwide thermonuclear war, in which even the fruits of victory would be ashes in our mouths," but he quickly added, "…neither shall we shrink from that risk if it must be faced."

The president enumerated his responses and demands, citing seven points:

1. That a naval "quarantine" would be placed around a section of the island to prevent any ships from delivering weaponry to Cuba. The use of the term 'quarantine,' coined by Theodore Roosevelt, carried significant legal weight, because calling it what it truly was – a naval blockade - is normally taken as an act of war. With the use of the gentler term, Kennedy cited the United Nation's Charter giving regions to the right to amass regional defenses. His exact words on this point were, "To halt this offensive buildup, a strict quarantine on all offensive military equipment under shipment to Cuba is being initiated. All ships of any kind bound for Cuba, from whatever nation or port, will, if found to contain cargoes of offensive weapons, be turned back. This quarantine will be extended, if needed, to other types of cargo and carriers. We are not at this time, however, denying the necessities of life as the Soviets attempted to do in their Berlin blockade of 1948."

2. That the island of Cuba would undergo continued and heightened surveillance, based on historical meetings of the Organization of American States (the OAS) rejecting secrecy in such important matters.

3. That any attack on a nation of South, Central or North America, no matter which one, would be taken as an attack on the United States by the Soviet Union and would receive the harshest response. Kennedy's exact words on this point were, "It shall be the policy of this nation to regard any nuclear missile launched from Cuba against any nation in the Western Hemisphere as an attack by the Soviet Union on the United States, requiring a full retaliatory response upon the Soviet Union."

4. That the base at Guantanamo had been immediately reinforced. In addition, history tells us that a sizeable troop movement by the United States sent reinforcements to southern states and coasts as well.

5. President Kennedy called for an immediate meeting of the appropriate sub-group with the OAS to discuss the situation, and to bring articles 6 and 8 of the Rio Treaty into effect. Also called the Inter-American Treaty of Reciprocal Assistance, article 6 addresses a threat without armed attack, mandating that "the Organ of

Consultation shall meet immediately in order to agree on the measures which must be taken in case of aggression to assist the victim of the aggression." Article 8 creates boundaries for what actions may be taken by member states, such as "recall of chiefs of diplomatic missions; breaking of diplomatic relations; breaking of consular relations; partial or complete interruption of economic relations; or of rail, sea, air, postal, telegraphic, telephonic and radiotelephonic or radiotelegraphic communications; and use of armed force."

6. He also called for an immediate convening of the United Nations Security Council.

7. The seventh point was directed at Premier Khrushchev himself, demanding that he "halt and eliminate this clandestine, reckless and provocative threat to world peace," and to "abandon his course of world domination," a calculated swipe at the larger revolutionary Soviet intent.

Kennedy further warned Khrushchev in the broadcast that no action taken against any country with which the United States is associated around the world would be tolerated, particularly in the city of West Berlin. Mention of Berlin was specifically important for the fact that Cuba was not truly what the Soviets wanted in the grand scheme of things; gaining a foothold in Berlin and points farther west would have suited their tastes much better.

At last addressing the Cuban people, and reminding all that he could be heard through specific radio broadcasts due to requests for air time made of nine stations, Kennedy referred to the entire leadership of the island as non-Cuban. Instead, he referred to the Castro regime as Soviet puppets and let the Cubans know theirs was the first country in their region to be the target of potential nuclear war or to have nuclear weapons on their home soil.

In the immediate wake of the president's address, Newsweek's poll revealed that almost 90% of the country opposed an invasion, except in the Midwest, where a "new belligerency" was taking hold. Construction of private fallout shelters increased, and students from elementary through secondary levels underwent regular drills to prepare for a nuclear attack. The stark Soviet presence may have been an added horror to the average American citizen, but the Soviet relationship with Cuba was certainly no surprise after 1961. Following the Bay of Pigs failure, the Senate, before the first recess, voted 86 – 1 to "stop the advance of communism in the Western Hemisphere." In fact, the Cuban question in general became perfect fodder for the Republicans in the mid-term elections, which were just a few weeks away. Kennedy was painted as an ineffective head of state, and tougher measures were called for across the Republican board. In clear evidence that the growing forces in Cuba were not necessarily hot-off-the-press revelations, *Newsweek* ran an article on October 15th asking, "What to do About the Arms Build-up in Cuba?" In fact, naval blockades were recommended that day from more than one legislative direction, and Kennedy was being labeled "tragically irresolute." What was news, however, was Soviet assistance in the buildup of weaponry on Cuba, and the presence of deliverable nuclear warheads so close to the American coast. In this, any last illusions of American isolationism were obliterated.

Chapter 11: Implementing the Blockade and Reacting to It

On October 23, the day after the broadcast, Kennedy signed Proclamation 3504, formally authorizing a quarantine of Cuba. In reference to the 26 Soviet ships already confirmed crossing the Atlantic, he distributed express orders: "No shooting without my explicit orders." On the same day, the Organization of American States approved a resolution for the immediate removal of the missiles. With that, the next few days would be spent mostly in secret meetings, as the American government agonized over a variety of potential responses, in particular what to do if and when the Soviet ships arrived. At the same time, the Administration was already considering the possibility of trading the removal of the missiles in Turkey and Italy for the removal of missiles in Cuba, information that was relayed to the U.S. Ambassador in Turkey and U.S. Ambassador to NATO.

Kennedy signing the Proclamation

For its part, the quarantine was put in place quickly, by October 24th, and the Kennedy administration had "the U.S. nuclear force placed on DEFCON 2 for the first and only time in history." U.S. Navy and Marine personnel were told on October 24 that their active duty could be extended for up to a year, and Washington sources reported over news outlets that "the first Russian ship to be intercepted might be the *Polatavia*, apparently designed to carry missiles." They added that the freighter was, by all accounts, unescorted. The Soviets also cancelled military leaves, and a curfew was put into effect for the British garrison in Berlin. That same day, Khrushchev sent a letter to Kennedy warning that the quarantine was "an act of aggression" and that it would be ignored, but American patrol planes that flew sorties near Soviet airspace as a result of DEFCON 2 noted that the Soviets didn't seem to be raising their own levels of alertness, as though nothing was going on. This led Air Force General David Burchinal to note "the Russians were so thoroughly stood down, and we knew it. They didn't make any move. They did not increase their alert; they did not increase any flights, or their air defense posture. They didn't do a thing, they froze in place." Burchinal claimed that the Soviet inaction led him to believe "we were never further from nuclear war than at the time of Cuba…" For his part, Kennedy responded to Khrushchev's letter by explaining that the placement of nuclear weapons in Cuba "required the responses I have announced … I hope that your government will take necessary action to permit a restoration of the earlier situation."

Of course, the Kennedy Administration was not so sure. The rapidly assembled naval force sent to execute the blockade naturally came from the lower East Coast and Caribbean, but it also involved numerous craft, air and support forces from some distance. Commander Task Force 136 from Virginia sent the *Newport News, Canberra, Lawrence, Keith, Soley* and *Borie* from Norfolk. The Commander-Cruiser-Destroyer Flotilla Six sent the *MacDonough* from Charleston. The Destroyer 26 of Norfolk sent several vessels, with some from Mayport as well. The Carrier *Essex* sailed out of Guantanamo. Four ships from Newport, and the Anti-Submarine Warfare Force at Roosevelt Roads and Bermuda were sent out for aircraft submarine surveillance. The *Monrovia, Rockbridge, Desoto County* and *Liddle* were sent to load a Marine Battalion Landing Team at Guantanamo, The *Capricornus* arrived at noon, and the *Lindenwald* by evening from North Carolina.

Submarine incursions represented a serious threat to the entire blockade, and in addition to American units in the Caribbean, navies of the U.K. and Canada were asked to assist. The U.S. also put out a call to the naval chiefs of Chile, Brazil, Colombia, Venezuela, Ecuador, Argentina, Uruguay and Peru. There was a more than reasonable expectation of assistance from the region, as the OAS resolution supporting the blockade had passed, 19–0.

The Essex group, under the control of McNamara and Admiral Robert Dennison, were instructed to halt the Soviet ships *Kimovsk* and *Gagarin* in the first group of interceptions. These ships had been well-located, and their current positions were fixed. The *Newport News, Canberra* and four destroyers were to intercept the *Polatavia*, and all intercepting groups were headed by a hunter/killer group for submarine attack prevention.

The quarantine line was laid out in a 500 mile arc from Cape Maysi, just outside the range of Soviet "Beagle" bombers already on the island, and the boarding policy and procedures were as follows:

1. The destroyer would give the "K" signal – (stop at once,) and would be given while out of position for the Soviet vessel to execute a ramming maneuver.

2. If the vessel did not stop, warning shots would be fired over the bow

3. If the vessel still refused, its non-vital parts could be targeted and damaged

4. Russian-trained linguists would join each boarding party

5. Manifest and cargo was to be inspected – if such inspection was refused, the ship would be taken into custody.

6. If there was organized resistance, the vessel was to be destroyed.

7. Confiscated ships would be taken to Charleston, San Juan, Roosevelt Roads or Fort Lauderdale

According to naval records, "another point discussed was the desirability of intercepting and searching ships that have reversed course and were proceeding eastward across the Atlantic. The final decision was not to intercept these ships, but to continue surveillance and make every effort to get good photographs of them and their deck cargoes."

As the Soviet ships made their way toward he blockade, the Soviets had to come up with their own response, and Khrushchev had his share of diverse opinions within the Kremlin. The Soviet Ambassador to Cuba, Alexander Alexeev, had become the primary Soviet confidant to Castro, and he accepted the Cuban leader's belief that the U.S. would strike Cuba in the near future as a rational possibility. Passing along Castro's seeming certainty to Khrushchev, Alexeev recommended an immediate preemptive nuclear and conventional strike against the United States, essentially calling for all-out war. Though outwardly belligerent himself, Khrushchev found such an action to be utterly reckless and rejected it out of hand.

Conversely, Andrei Gromyko, the Soviet Foreign Minister, had opposed the missile installations from the beginning and was preoccupied with American reaction. When he met with Kennedy on more than one occasion, he was unaware that the American president knew what was happening in Cuba, and he maintained the position that the weapons were solely defensive. Meanwhile, the Deputy Minister, Anasatas Mikoyan, recommended a counter-blockade with intense pressure brought to bear against Berlin. While Rodion Malinovsky, a top Soviet military officer, supported and managed first-hand all matters of military assistance to Cuba, he also generally opposed Khrushchev's strategy.

Perhaps most incredibly, the Soviet Ambassador to the United States, Alexander Dobrynin, was not informed by his leadership of the missile situation at all, but ultimately, his secret series of meetings with Robert Kennedy provided the perfect cover for conversations between Kennedy and Khrushchev. It was during these meetings that the removal of the Jupiter missiles from Turkey and Italy was first discussed between the two sides.

Regardless of internal deliberations, Khrushchev seemed not to have been caught off guard by the blockade, and he quickly instructed Soviet ships to proceed quickly to the quarantine line. On

October 24, two days after the Kennedy broadcast, the first Soviet ships reached the quarantine line and received radio instructions from Moscow not to attempt crossing it but to hold position.

As that was going on, Bobby Kennedy, possibly the most well-informed of all the advisors due to a spate of secret meetings with parties from both countries and possessing the constant ear of the president, reported that Georgy Bolshakov of the Soviet Embassy believed Khrushchev would instruct his ships to break the blockade, no matter what the American response. His rationale for such a belief was that "this is a defensive base for the Russians. It's got nothing to do with the Cubans." Meanwhile, McNamara also worried about the additional danger of the quarantine line being "shadowed" by Soviet submarines, which had been located off the East Coast of the U.S. before and were known to be difficult to counteract with their nuclear capabilities.

With Soviet ships at the quarantine line, the president also had to deal with what to do about those ships. Sensitive to public opinion, Kennedy, again to the consternation of military chiefs, addressed the question of stopping, boarding and inspecting ships not loaded with illegal materials and recommended that no action above the standard inspection be taken against a ship that acts in accordance with the blockade. For the moment, Kennedy was able to break the tension in the room by cautioning against confiscating and towing in a Soviet ship, only to find that it was filled with baby food.

Chapter 12: An International Response

Whether the crisis would produce a war or not, there was a separate battle to be won that would almost certainly affect foreign relations for a prolonged period of time, and that was the tide of international opinion. In a sense, international perception over which side actually won the standoff carried as much if not more gravity than the reality of the outcome.

Uruguay had abstained from the OAS vote due to lack of instructions, reserving the right to add its vote later, but no serious objections to the proceedings were voiced. Japan's entire air defense was put on alert, and Chancellor Adenauer backed the U.S. position openly. While Canadian Prime Minister Diefenbaker agreed with the American president's assessment of the situation, he did not comment on the blockade itself. Charles de Gaulle instructed France's United Nations delegation to follow the German lead and support the American position. As expected, the Pacific nations of South Vietnam, Philippines, South Korea and Nationalist China (Formosa – Taiwan) backed the U.S. decision, while communist blocs and their satellites uniformly supported the Soviet stance.

Russian journalists in Europe and Asia predicted widespread war if one single Soviet ship was sunk, and they opined that the Soviets were itching for such a test of strength with the U.S., a test it heartily believed it could win. Contrary to that, however, no intelligence reports whatsoever remarked on any extraordinary troop movements or unusual preparations for conflict in either the central Soviet bloc or any of its surrounding states.

After Kennedy had called for a convening of the Security Council, U.S. Ambassador Stevenson made a presentation before the council on October 25. Kennedy had procured an excellent mouthpiece to serve as ambassador to the United Nations in Adlai Stevenson. A governor of Illinois and two-time presidential candidate, he was known for his somewhat stolid public presentation. However, in taking the photographic evidence to the General Assembly, Stevenson created quite a furor by almost waving the photos in the face of the Russian ambassador Valerian Zorn, in an attempt to force the Soviet official to admit the existence of the missiles before the world community.

Stevenson showing the pictures to the council.

With the American leadership looking for signs of more aggressive or cautious movement from their Soviet counterparts, one informative impression occurred at the Security Council, where the Soviet Ambassador, Valerian Zorin, replied to Stevenson's presentation:

> "When Mr. Stevenson today attempted to accuse the Soviet Union as the prime cause for these aggressive actions on the part of the United States, I should like to draw attention of the Council to a completely surprising fact.
>
> In the statement of President Kennedy of the 22nd of October, Mr. Kennedy said that during the last week unmistakable evidence has established the fact that a series

of offensive missile sites is now in preparation on that island.

On the 16th of October the President of the United States had in his hands incontrovertible information. What happened after that? On the 18th of October the President of the United States was receiving the representative of the Soviet Union, the Minister of Foreign Affairs, Mr. Gromyko, two days after he had already in his hands incontrovertible evidence.

One may well ask why did the President of the United States in receiving the minister of another power which the Government of the United States is now accusing of dispatching offensive arms to Cuba against the United States, why then did he not say a word to the Minister of Foreign Affairs of the Soviet Union with respect to these incontrovertible facts?

Why? Because no such facts exist. The Government of the United States has no such fact in its hands except these falsified information of the United States Intelligence Agency, which are being displayed for review in halls and which are sent to the press.

Falsity is what the United States has in its hands, false evidence.

The Government of the United States has deliberately intensified the crisis, has deliberately prepared this provocation and had tried to cover up this provocation by means of a discussion in the Security Council.

You cannot conduct world policies and politics on such an opportunistic matter. Such steps can lead you to catastrophic consequences for the whole world, and the Soviet Government has issued a warning to the United States and to the world on that score.

The Soviet Union considers that the Government of the United States of America must display reserve and stay the execution of its piratical threats, which are fraught with the most serious consequence.

The question of war and peace is so vital that we should consider useful a top level meeting in order to discuss all the problems which have arisen to do everything to remove the danger of unleashing a thermonuclear war."

However, the normally belligerent Soviet mode of public expression softened considerably, and by all appearances, the Soviet Ambassador seemed to be bending over backward to avoid a full conflict. This seemed to coincide with the fact that the Soviet ships were proceeding with extreme caution; even on the morning of October 24, the first signs began to appear that some Soviet ships were slowing down and others were turning around. Secretary McNamara would not receive this news for the next three hours, but the president received it very quickly and immediately instructed military leadership that it was not to be leaked to the press under any circumstances, beginning with General Taylor and Admiral Anderson. When U.N. Secretary General U. Thant announced the recommendation of a "cooling off" period, Khrushchev immediately accepted it but Kennedy flatly refused.

Chapter 13: Finding a Way Out of the Crisis

Back in the Caribbean, the tension shifted somewhat from those dangers that could be seen to those that could not. Secretary of Defense McNamara remained preoccupied with locating and shadowing Soviet submarines, and for good reason, considering their advanced technology in battle and "quiet running." He requested from the Naval Department an effective method of signaling an enemy submarine to surface, presumably for search and/or surrender. American ship and land communications were not entirely compatible with undersea Soviet communication systems, so the more primitive method of dropping a depth charge, much like a shot across the bow, was adopted. Although it would only be discovered decades after the crisis, Soviet subs had been ordered to launch their nuclear missiles if a depth charge breached its hull and was about to sink it. When Navy ships dropped depth charges near one Soviet sub, the officers on board debated whether to fire the nuclear missiles onboard. Launching them required a unanimous vote, but 1 of the 3 rejected the notion. In reference to that, Thomas Blanton, the director of the National Security Archive, once commented, "A guy called Vasili Arkhipov saved the world."

Two additional incidents were, for a time, troubling to those on the ships themselves. Contact with the Soviet ship *Bucharest* was lost, and she was eventually relocated again by the Essex group inside of the interception line. Pursued by *Newport News* and *Gearing*, the latter flashed a signal for the *Bucharest* to stop and identify herself. The reply came: "My name is Bucharest, Russian ship from the Black Sea, bound for Cuba." *Gearing* flashed another message, beginning the most courteous exchange of the entire crisis. The message was simply, "Good morning." The reply was, "Good morning, thank you." The *Bucharest* was not fully boarded, but it had topside photos taken, and with no evidence of illegal items, she was cleared and allowed to continue.

While it was certainly not the defining moment of the Cuban Missile Crisis, the boarding and release of the *Bucharest* brought about a general sigh of relief in America, perhaps because it was the first overtly visible sign of the affair they were allowed to see and read about. Almost instantly, "the stock market edged back up; the man on the street appeared anxious but supportive; while press editorials also conveyed support."

McNamara's fear of Soviet submarines was not overblown, and several were located on the 25th, even as some Russian cargo ships were turning around. Out of the estimated number of ships approaching the line, nine either reversed or in some way altered course east of the line. Although six were still close to crossing the line, seven more to the east also reversed course, and three more turned around the next day. Even still, four submarines were detected within the interception area and could still inflict damage without the surface flotilla. While American forces tagged and followed those, two more Soviet subs were located off of Haiti and the Dominican Republic.

The numerous identifications of Soviet submarines forced several of them to surface under pressure of surveillance, but there were no surface inspections of the subs, in part because attention had been turned to other matters. From a military standpoint, emphasis began to shift in the American leadership toward the invasion of Cuba, which would have been an amphibious Naval/Marine action in large force, along with extending the quarantine to stop all ships sailing under all flags headed to Cuba, even those currently passing through the Panama Canal. While Soviet ships turned and submarines were identified, work on the land installations in Cuba went ahead with no hesitation. The degree of knowledge of which they were privy to the day's events was unknown, but Castro had certainly not accepted any foregone conclusion about Soviet retreat and proceeded as planned.

An American helicopter hovering over a Soviet submarine

By now, however, there were plenty of back-channel communications going on as both sides attempted to figure out a way to end the crisis while saving face. On the afternoon of October 26, John Scali, a journalist for ABC, met with a Russian KGB contact who urged him to approach American officials about a deal that would see the missiles in Cuba removed in exchange for American assurances never to invade the island. While the Administration was not yet willing to deal in such absolute terms, they passed a message through Brazil to Castro suggesting the U.S. would be "unlikely to invade" if the missiles were removed.

Scali

On a more formal level, Khrushchev sent a message to Kennedy on the evening of the 26th that suggested he was willing to negotiate:

> "Mr. President, we and you ought not now to pull on the ends of the rope in which you have tied the knot of war, because the more the two of us pull, the tighter that knot will be tied. And a moment may come when that knot will be tied so tight that even he who tied it will not have the strength to untie it, and then it will be necessary to cut that knot, and what that would mean is not for me to explain to you, because you yourself understand perfectly of what terrible forces our countries dispose.
>
> Consequently, if there is no intention to tighten that knot and thereby to doom the world to the catastrophe of thermonuclear war, then let us not only relax the forces

pulling on the ends of the rope, let us take measures to untie that knot. We are ready for this."

Though it would later be determined that the KGB contact had approached Scali without any guidance from the Kremlin, Khrushchev's letter also seemed to outline the parameters that Scali and his contact had discussed earlier that afternoon: "I propose: we, for our part, will declare that our ships bound for Cuba are not carrying any armaments. You will declare that the United States will not invade Cuba with its troops and will not support any other forces which might intend to invade Cuba. Then the necessity of the presence of our military specialists in Cuba will disappear."

Before the Administration came up with a formal response to Khrushchev's communication on the 26th, he suggested a different deal early on the 27th. This time, Khrushchev suggested that the Jupiter missiles in Turkey be removed: "You are disturbed over Cuba. You say that this disturbs you because it is ninety-nine miles by sea from the coast of the United States of America. But ... you have placed destructive missile weapons, which you call offensive, in Italy and Turkey, literally next to us ... I therefore make this proposal: We are willing to remove from Cuba the means which you regard as offensive ... Your representatives will make a declaration to the effect that the United States ... will remove its analogous means from Turkey ... and after that, persons entrusted by the United Nations Security Council could inspect on the spot the fulfillment of the pledges made."

Given that this message was materially different than the message from the night before, it muddled the exchange and left Washington wondering if Khrushchev had been swayed by hard-liners or if he had even possibly been overthrown. At the same time, Kennedy was aware that the terms of this offer had all but boxed him in and precluded any military action because it would be considered a reasonable offer internationally. Since the Jupiter missiles in Turkey were obsolete and would be removed at some point soon anyway, Kennedy noted "it's gonna – to any man at the United Nations or any other rational man, it will look like a very fair trade." Turkey's government was upset about the possibility that the missiles would be removed throughout the crisis, but the Italians were willing to have the missiles stationed there used as a bargaining chip.

Just when it looked like a breakthrough was forthcoming, a calamity occurred on the 27th. On that day, an Alaskan U-2 strayed into eastern Soviet airspace, and was chased away by fighters. A subsequent letter from Khrushchev did not mention the incident specifically, but he warned the U.S. that any major mishaps with U-2s over Russia could result in nuclear war. However, on the afternoon of the very same day, a Cuban SAM successfully shot down a U-2 plane and killed the pilot, and when that news reached Kennedy, it immediately threw everything into flux. Initially, it was reported that ground forces in Cuba had fired on "hostile aircraft," and one U-2 was by this time an hour late in arriving at its landing base. The protocol for such a loss included a strike on the offending installation, and 131 aircraft were positioned from five states from as far west as Nevada.

By 3:30 that same afternoon, the Pentagon released a statement that the Jupiter missiles had been installed in Turkey as part of a NATO Council Resolution and could therefore not be removed. By this time, two more U-2s had been fired at by the Cubans, and one plane was still confirmed missing. Castro, whether out of the loop of messages going back and forth between the two superpowers, or not interested in the direction of the agenda, contacted the American State Department and staunchly refused to allow the dismantling of the missile installations, and based on this (and a possible impending invasion), the military brass urged adding oil to the prohibited list for any ship headed to Cuba.

Confirmation came quickly that one of the U-2s had been shot down by a SAM, and many involved believed it to be the worst moment of the crisis. Dino Brugione, a CIA photo analyst, reported, "It was a day of horrors…we could have stumbled into World War III very easily." The pilot, who ended up being the only casualty of the crisis, was Major Rudolf Anderson, who was flying his sixth mission over Cuba and knew the SAMs were operational.

Anderson

Robert Kennedy, in his seminal book about the crisis, *Thirteen Days*, explained that after the death of Anderson, "There was a feeling that the noose was tightening on all of us, on Americans, on mankind, and that bridges to escape were crumbling." At the same time, he later defended the missions: "We had to send a U-2 over to gain reconnaissance information on whether the Soviet missiles were becoming operational. We believed that if the U-2 was shot down that - the Cubans didn't have capabilities to shoot it down, the Soviets did - we believed if it was shot down, it would be shot down by a Soviet surface-to-air-missile unit, and that it would represent a decision by the Soviets to escalate the conflict. And therefore, before we sent the U-2 out, we agreed that if it was shot down we wouldn't meet, we'd simply attack. It was shot down on Friday. ... Fortunately, we changed our mind, we thought 'Well, it might have been an accident, we won't attack.' Later we learned that Khrushchev had reasoned just as we did: we send over the U-2, if it was shot down, he reasoned we would believe it was an intentional escalation. And therefore, he issued orders to Pliyev, the Soviet commander in Cuba, to instruct all of his batteries not to shoot down the U-2."

The possibility of all-out war was now closer than ever, but Kennedy ultimately (and correctly) presumed that the order to fire had not come from the Soviets. Around the same time, Khrushchev was also rebuffing Castro's suggestion of resorting to nuclear war; Castro had written to him in a letter on the 27th, "I believe the imperialists' aggressiveness is extremely dangerous and if they actually carry out the brutal act of invading Cuba in violation of international law and morality, that would be the moment to eliminate such danger forever through an act of clear legitimate defense, however harsh and terrible the solution would be." Instead, the two sides stepped back, providing an important lesson about the (lack of) wisdom of letting third parties possess weapons that would implicate and affect larger nations.

Later on the 27th, American and Soviet intermediaries met for dinner, and President Kennedy was prepared to accept Khrushchev's proposal, but he was talked into going back to the original offer of having the missiles removed in exchange for a promise not to invade Cuba. Kennedy's letter read, "As I read your letter, the key elements of your proposals—which seem generally acceptable as I understand them - are as follows: 1) You would agree to remove these weapons systems from Cuba under appropriate United Nations observation and supervision; and undertake, with suitable safe-guards, to halt the further introduction of such weapon systems into Cuba. 2) We, on our part, would agree—upon the establishment of adequate arrangements through the United Nations, to ensure the carrying out and continuation of these commitments (a) to remove promptly the quarantine measures now in effect and (b) to give assurances against the invasion of Cuba."

Meanwhile, Bobby Kennedy, who had been secretly meeting with Soviet officials, including the Soviet Ambassador to the U.S., gave an identical copy to Ambassador Dobrynin with the warning that an attack on Cuba would commence in the next 24 hours unless the Soviets responded immediately. Bobby later remembered, "We had not abandoned all hope, but what hope there was now rested with Khrushchev's revising his course within the next few hours. It was a hope, not an expectation. The expectation was military confrontation…" McNamara explained what would be necessary for military planning in the event of a military action: "a government for Cuba, because we're going to need one; and secondly, plans for how to respond to the Soviet Union in Europe, because sure as hell they're going to do something there."

Ultimately, by the end of the 27th, a secret deal was in place that had Soviet missiles removed from Cuba in exchange for the removal of the missiles in Italy and Turkey, along with a promise not to invade Cuba. With that, Khrushchev ordered the missile sites dismantled on the 28th of October, and sent another letter to Kennedy to that effect, asking that the U.S. stop the flights over Cuba. Part of the letter read, "the Soviet government, in addition to previously issued instructions on the cessation of further work at the building sites for the weapons, has issued a new order on the dismantling of the weapons which you describe as 'offensive' and their crating and return to the Soviet Union." However, any cause for celebration was immediately stifled, because the proposal was rife with loopholes and much verification would be necessary to see that the promise was fulfilled in its entirety. Nevertheless, Kennedy quickly responded, "I consider my letter to you of October twenty-seventh and your reply of today as firm undertakings on the part of both our governments which should be promptly carried out … The US will make a statement in the framework of the Security Council in reference to Cuba as follows: it will declare that the United States of America will respect the inviolability of Cuban borders, its sovereignty, that it take the pledge not to interfere in internal affairs, not to intrude themselves and not to permit our territory to be used as a bridgehead for the invasion of Cuba, and will restrain those who would plan to carry an aggression against Cuba, either from US territory or from the territory of other countries neighboring to Cuba."

Chapter 14: The Aftermath of the Crisis

Picture of an EXCOMM meeting on October 29

Nobody suffered more politically from the end of the crisis than Khrushchev, who was viewed by the Communist bloc as having backed down almost entirely. This was due in part to the fact the terms of the deal were secret, most notably the removal of missiles in Turkey; as Alexander Dobrynin noted, it was Khrushchev's "failure to insist on a public pledge to swap Turkish for Cuban missiles by Kennedy that cost him dearly." Kennedy walked away from the crisis having been perceived the winner, and Khrushchev, who had attained the missile reduction and protected Cuba long-term, was perceived as the humiliated party. Naturally, Khrushchev's impression of Kennedy changed considerably after the crisis, and he commented in memoirs that "one must have a sober-minded counterpart with whom to deal". In this way, he complimented Kennedy for being trustworthy and capable of understanding the situation well. At the same time, given the sheer amount of correspondence and phone calls between Washington and Moscow, either direct or through the embassies during the conflict, it became clear to all parties that a lapse of accessibility in mutual communications could have caused the crisis to end badly. As a result, the infamous "hot line," a Washington-to-Moscow phone connection, was established for quick responses and confirmations.

Of course, none of this was enough to save Khrushchev politically. Though he signed the first test ban treaty between the Soviet Union, the United States and the United Kingdom in July 1963, his political career was already over, even if Khrushchev himself wasn't yet aware of it.

While Khrushchev was away from Moscow in the early months of 1964, conspirators began plotting to remove him from power. That March, Supreme Soviet head Leonid Brezhnev began planning for a removal of Khrushchev from power with a bunch of other party officials, with the plot ranging from an arrest to a simple ouster.

The conspirators, led by Brezhnev, Aleksandr Shelepin, and KGB Chairman Vladimir Semichastny, put their plan into action in October, while Khrushchev was on vacation. On October 12, 1963, Brezhnev called Khrushchev and let him know about a special Presidium meeting to discuss agriculture, though Khrushchev himself now began to understand what was up. When he arrived in Moscow, Khrushchev faced condemnation from Brezhnev and others for his failures, to which he didn't fight. That night, he explained to his Presidium colleague Anastas Mikoyan, "I'm old and tired. Let them cope by themselves. I've done the main thing. Could anyone have dreamed of telling Stalin that he didn't suit us anymore and suggesting he retire? Not even a wet spot would have remained where we had been standing. Now everything is different. The fear is gone, and we can talk as equals. That's my contribution. I won't put up a fight."

Thus, Khrushchev faced no other choice but to retire as both First Secretary and Premier. Brezhnev immediately replaced him as First Secretary, and Alexei Kosygin became the new premier.

Khrushchev wasn't the only political loser. A frustrated Castro, left without support of the Soviet Union and still anticipating an American invasion of Cuba, channeled his fury into exhortations for widespread acts of terrorism within Latin America, from urging Hondurans to overthrow their government to a call for attacks on the oil fields of Venezuela. Nevertheless, from October 29-31, initial actions were taken to stop installation construction, and by November, the missiles and installations were removed from the island. In the years since, as the Soviet Union's structure deteriorated and Russia moved toward a more free-market economy, Cuba has not budged from its 1962 position. In retrospect, it was Castro's feeling that with all the construction and chicken farms in Cuba, the missile installations could have been more successfully camouflaged with ease and would not been discovered until much later. Even after decades of hindsight, he nevertheless clings to an insistence that one cannot cower before a larger enemy, even with a sudden loss of support from a trusted ally: "As we began to lose faith in the Soviet policy, we began to change our tactics…we realized how alone we would be in the event of war. We also realized how stupid it was to withdraw those troops in the face of an enemy that demanded it, and that would in future years further aggravate our perilous situation."

True to the agreement, the United States never mounted another military action against the Castro regime, but it remained quick to embrace, quietly or publicly, any sentiment from within that threatened to destabilize it. Travel and trade between the island and America was severed, with some softening only coming about during the Obama administration. Likewise, Castro never again embraced another communist bloc power in the way he had the Soviets. In declining health, he has transferred some authority to his brother, Raul.

On the other hand, despite the foreign policy failures of Kennedy's first year and a half in office, the Cuban Missile Crisis significantly increased the Administration's credibility on foreign policy matters. By fending off Soviet aggression, Kennedy renewed the America's commitment to defending the Western Hemisphere and repositioned the nation with strength. Prior to the crisis, the Soviets had viewed the Kennedy Administration as weak, but by averting nuclear war and removing the Soviet missiles from Cuba, Kennedy's political popularity improved, and he was again lauded for his foreign policy achievements. Now seemingly finding his stride, in June 1963, Kennedy traveled to West Berlin, where he gave his famous Berlin Wall Speech. In it, he said, "All free men, wherever they may live, are citizens of Berlin, and, therefore, as a free man, I take pride in the words: Ich bin ein Berliner." In the speech, Kennedy reiterated the American commitment to Berlin and West Germany. It was very well received by Germans, and it helped to solidify the alignment of Western Europe with the United States against the Soviets.

Chapter 15: The Cuban Missile Crisis in Hindsight

Still one of the most studied episodes in American history, the Cuban Missile Crisis is occasionally an object of a reference even now, and it can cause heated arguments within government seminars. That said, most American figures of the two major parties at least minimally saluted the Kennedy Administration's handling of the situation that October, albeit with varying degrees of reservations. President Ronald Reagan used the event as a comparison to his own time, contrasting Kennedy's difficulties as being far easier than his own: "At the time of the Cuban missile crisis…it had been relatively easy to stand up to the Soviets."

Whether all those present in 1962 would have agreed is open to question. As historian Graham Allison recently put it: "Fifty years ago, the Cuban missile crisis brought the world to the brink of nuclear disaster. During the standoff, US President John F. Kennedy thought the chance of escalation to war was 'between 1 in 3 and even,' and what we have learned in later decades has done nothing to lengthen those odds. We now know, for example, that in addition to nuclear-armed ballistic missiles, the Soviet Union had deployed 100 tactical nuclear weapons to Cuba, and the local Soviet commander there could have launched these weapons without additional codes or commands from Moscow. The US air strike and invasion that were scheduled for the third week of the confrontation would likely have triggered a nuclear response against American ships and troops, and perhaps even Miami. The resulting war might have led to the deaths of 100 million Americans and over 100 million Russians." While those tactical nukes had gone unnoticed by American intelligence, the Soviets eventually removed them from Cuba because they didn't personally trust Castro and thus refused to let him have access to such powerful weaponry. Those weapons were removed from Cuba by the Soviets in December 1962.

Looking at the long-term losses and gains from that era, Zbigniew Brezinski, the National Security Advisor for the Carter Administration, gave a gloomy appraisal. "Even in the one instance where the United States acted like a great power – the Cuban missile crisis in 1962 – it failed to harvest the fruits of its effort. The United States did not exploit the success either to pressure the Soviet Union to withdraw from the Caribbean through an arrangement for the full neutralization of Cuba, or to structure a more stable and more cooperative relationship with the Soviet Union…instead, we deluded ourselves with the comfortable belief…that the Soviet Union had accommodated itself indefinitely to strategic inferiority."

In a different line of criticism, Curtis LeMay continued insisting the Cuban Missile Crisis was "the greatest defeat in our history." 25 years after the Crisis, he still claimed, "We could have gotten not only the missiles out of Cuba, we could have gotten the Communists out of Cuba at that time."

However, many other scholars look upon the administration's response in 1962 with favor, pointing out that it was not possible to solve all the larger problems in an intense two-week period and that handling the specific crisis, which had precipitated itself in such a short time no less, was the overriding concern. Indeed, it's important to remember that the Cuban Missile Crisis was just one facet of the ongoing Cold War. The ongoing rivalry between the two superpowers could not possibly have been solved in two weeks, and the added unstable presence of Castro increased the delicacy of the situation several-fold.

In general, most historians have looked favorably upon the Kennedy Administration's actions during the Cuban Missile Crisis, and in the weeks and months following the crisis, Kennedy "embarked on months of negotiations to try to draw a line under the crisis, to restore the situation to a status quo ante, and to remove the issue as a nuclear flash point." By 1963, the first agreement was signed to limit the testing of nuclear devices, and the habit of secretly taping all meetings, phone calls, and other communications continued, due to the great assistance the practice had been throughout the crisis. Kennedy enjoyed higher popular ratings than any other president after the crisis, but poll numbers gradually slipped from the high 70s to the low 60s over the course of several weeks. The resolution to the missile crisis sent his numbers shooting up for a short while, and the next phase of his presidency, a considerably calmer one, is a largely overlooked phase of his presidency. As White House historian Arthur M. Schlesinger noted, until Kennedy's assassination in November 1963, the period after the missile crisis was fraught with far less criticism and "marked by a greater stability."

Bibliography

ABC News, JFK Tapes, New Insight into White House Tensions during Cuban Missile Crisis, Sept. 24, 2012

Belzer, Richard, "Lamentations and Regrets" - Huffington Post - www.huffingtonpost.com/richard-belzer

Blight, James G., Brenner, Philip, Harvard Kennedy School, Belfert Center, Sad and Luminous Days: Castro's Struggle with the Superpowers after the Missile Crisis (Fidel Castro's 'Secret Speech,' January 1968) Landon MD: Rowman and Littlefield Publishers, 2002

Bradley, William, "Why We Should Miss John F. Kennedy 50 Years On" - Huffington Post - www.huffingtonpost.com/william-bradley

Brown University, the Choices Program – Cuban Missile Crisis – www.choices.edu

CIA Official History of the Bay of Pigs Operation - www.paperlessarchives.com/bay-of-pigs-cia-history.html

Coleman, David G., The Fourteenth Day: JFK and the Aftermath of the Cuban Missile Crisis, Miller Center of Public Affairs, W.W. Norton: New York, 2012

Gleijeses, Piero, "Ships in the Night and the Bay of Pigs", in *Journal of Latin American Studies,* Vol. 27 No. 1, February 1995

Harvard Kennedy School, Belfer Center for Science and International Affairs – www.cubanmissilecrisis.org/lessons-key-documents

History.com - www.history.com/topics/bay-of-pigs-invasion

John. F. Kennedy Presidential Library and Museum – www.library.org/Cuban-missile-crisis, aspx.

Lynch, Grafton L., Central Intelligence - Bay of Pigs Release - Aug. 2, 2011 - www.foia.cia.gov/collection/bay-of-pigs-release

Lynch, Lieutenant Colonel Maureen M., USMC, GlobalSecurityOrg – Cuba, Castro and the Cuban Missile Crisis, April 3, 1995 – www.globalsecurity.org/wmd/library/report/Thesis/1995

Marfleet, Gregory, "The Operational Code of John F. Kennedy during the Cuban Missile Crisis: A Comparison of Public and Private Rhetoric", in Political Psychology Vol. 21 No. 3, Sept. 2000

National Security Archives, the George Washington University - www2.gwu.edu/nsarchiv./NSAEBB29/index.htm

Naval History & Heritage, the Naval Quarantine of Cuba, 1962 – www.history.navy.mil

Netplaces – John F. Kennedy, Meeting with Khrushchev – www.netplaces.com/john-f-kennedy/meeting-with-khrushchev.htm

Pérez, Luis, Jr., "Fear and Loathing of Fidel Castro: Sources of U.S. Policy toward Cuba", in *Journal of Latin American Studies,* Vol. 34 No. 3, May 2002

Pohlmann, Marcus D., "Constraining Presidents at the Brink", in Presidential Studies Quarterly, Vol. 19 No. 2 (Spring 1989)

Public Resource Org – www.youtube.org

Rumbaut, Luis E., Rubén G., "Survivor: Cuba: The Cuban Revolution at 50", in *Latin American Perspectives,* Vol. 36 No. 1, January 2009

RussianSpaceWeb.com, Soviet Archives, Cuba, 1962 – www.russianspaceweb.com

Sandman, Joshua H., "Analyzing Foreign Policy Crisis Situations: The Bay of Pigs", in *Presidential Studies Quarterly,* Vol. 16 No. 2, Spring, 1986

Sierra. J.A. "Cuba in the 1960s: An Introduction" - www.historyofcuba.com/history/havana/sixties.htm

Sierra, J.A., The Cuba Missile Crisis – a timeline, historyofcuba.com

Swift, John, History Today, the Cuban Missile Crisis – www.historytoday.com

The Baltimore Sun, Downing of U.S. Spy Plane in Cuba Turned Hot Crisis Feverish 30 Years Ago, Sept. 1994

The Guardian.com, World News Wednesday 24 October 1962: 25 Soviet Ships on Way to Cuba

This Day in Aviation – www.thisdayinaviation.com/14-october-1962

Thrall, Nathan, Wilkins, Jesse James, New York Times – Kennedy Talked, Khrushchev Triumphed, May 22, 2008

U.S. Department of State, Inter-American Treaty of Reciprocal Assistance – www.state.gov/p/wha/ris/70861.htm